Ireland

Louise Ní Chríodáin

Photography by Douglas Robertson

HarperCollins*Publishers*

Contents

Dublin

Preceding page: Custom House   Christ Church Cathedral

Bloomsday, Davy Byrne's (James Carney)

Though man has lived around Atha Cliatha ('the ford of the hurdles') since prehistoric times, and a number of monasteries were founded in the area, it was not until the arrival of the Vikings in AD 840 that a town of some size began to develop.

The Norsemen used Dublin as a base for both trade and raids, holding control of the area until their defeat at the Battle of Clontarf in 1014.

At the request of an ex-king of Leinster, Dermot McMurrough, a group of Norman mercenaries, following instructions from Henry II and led by 'Strongbow', captured much of Leinster, storming Dublin in 1169. Three years later King Henry decided the Normans were becoming too powerful and sent in a large army to subdue them. The town then became the bastion of English power over most of Leinster – the Pale.

At the peak of English control in Ireland during the 17thC, the city began to expand, and the 18thC saw the construction of what is now known as Georgian Dublin.

O'Connell Street

With the conceding of autonomy to the Irish Parliament in 1783, Dublin blossomed, but William Pitt, alarmed by the United Irishmen's rebellion in 1798, achieved the reunion of the parliaments in 1801.

By the end of the 19thC Dublin was a predominantly Irish town, and it became the centre for two important cultural movements: the Gaelic League (Conradh na Gaeilge), which promoted the revival of the Irish language; and the Irish Literary Renaissance, which continued into the 20thC and brought about the foundation of the Abbey Theatre.

The early part of this century saw the struggle to establish the trade union movement, culminating in the devastating Great Lock-out of 1913. The Easter Rising, War of Independence and Civil War all took their toll on the city but, as the capital of the Free State and later the Republic, it grew slowly until the economic upswing of the 1960s, when the population and business boomed.

Today's Dublin is attempting to recover from some disastrous planning decisions over the past 20 years, including sprawling, badly-serviced suburbs and even the building of two monstrous civic buildings over an extensive Viking site at Woodquay behind Christ Church. Projects like the development of the Temple Bar area – Dublin's 'Left Bank' – off Dame St are a start but there is still a long way to go.

Dublin's Civic Museum on South William St is a treasure-trove of newspapers, maps, posters, prints and other artefacts tracing the city's history. The Flame on the Hill, a visual presentation of Ireland's story before the Vikings, can be seen at St. Audoen's Church in High St, which was built on the old Dublin walls, which in turn were on the site of the city's first Viking settlement.

Among the many other historic buildings open to the public in Dublin are 18thC Newman House, site of Ireland's first Catholic university. Gerard Manley Hopkins, James Joyce and Brian Nolan (Flann O'Brien/Myles na gCopaleen) are

Above and below: Grafton Street

among its former students and teachers. St. Mary's Abbey Chapterhouse, situated off Capel St, founded in 1139 by the Benedictine order, is one of Ireland's largest and most historic monasteries. St. Michan's, founded by the Norsemen in 1095, is famous for the medieval mummified bodies in its vaults, and Handel performed his *Dettingen Te Deum* here; the organ which was used is on display.

Over the years one of Dublin's most renowned exports has been its writers and their works. This little city has been home, and the source of some of the inspiration, for a diverse list of authors, including Jonathan Swift, Oscar Wilde, J. M. Synge, Sean O'Casey, Brendan Behan, Patrick Kavanagh, George Bernard Shaw, J. P. Donleavy, Flann O'Brien, W. B. Yeats and Samuel Beckett. The tradition continues today and a first stop for information on the writers of the past and present is the Dublin Writers' Museum in Parnell Sq.

O'Connell Bridge

Dublin Castle

Grafton Street

The Long Room, Trinity College (James Carney)

For many people, however, Dublin more importantly is the source of one of the world's most famous beverages – Guinness. The first pint of Guinness porter or stout was 'sunk' in 1759 when Arthur Guinness founded his brewery at St. James's Gate on the River Liffey. Until 1939 it was the largest brewery in the world. Though now brewed in 16 other countries, the discerning Guinness drinker will swear it tastes best in Dublin. Drawing a pint is almost regarded as an art form, so expect a wait of a few minutes while the creamy head 'settles'. The Guinness Visitor Centre at the old hop store on Crane St includes a brewing museum, video show and a free sample of 'the black stuff'.

In a city where brewing has played a vital role, it is no surprise that another of Dublin's great attractions is its pubs, and there are plenty to choose from – over 800! The Brazen Head Inn is the city's oldest pub, licensed in 1666 but said to date from the 13thC, while the Stag's Head in

9

Above: Bewley's Oriental Café, Grafton Street

Below: Christ Church Cathedral Crypt

Dame Court was built in 1770, remodelled in 1895 and became one of the first pubs to get electricity. Ryan's of Parkgate St is virtually unchanged since the turn of the century, and there has been a pub on the site of O'Neill's in Suffolk St for over 300 years. For literary connections visit the Palace Bar, Fleet St; Mulligan's in Poolbeg St, which gets a mention in Joyce's *Dubliners*; Davy Byrne's in Duke St, where Leopold Bloom dined in *Ulysses*; McDaid's on Harry St, a favourite haunt of Brendan Behan; and Toner's, Lower Baggot St, the only pub reputed to have served W. B. Yeats! For music you won't do much better than O'Donoghue's on Merrion Row or An Beal Bocht on Charlemount St.

The city is also home to Bewley's Oriental Cafés which, like the pubs, are conducive to conversation and the whiling away of an hour or so. The original cafés in Grafton and Westmoreland streets are still the best in which to enjoy breakfast, the marvellous Bewley's coffee or afternoon tea, and watch the world pass by, which you can be sure is never at too quick a pace in Dublin.

Georgian Doorway, Guinness Visitor Centre

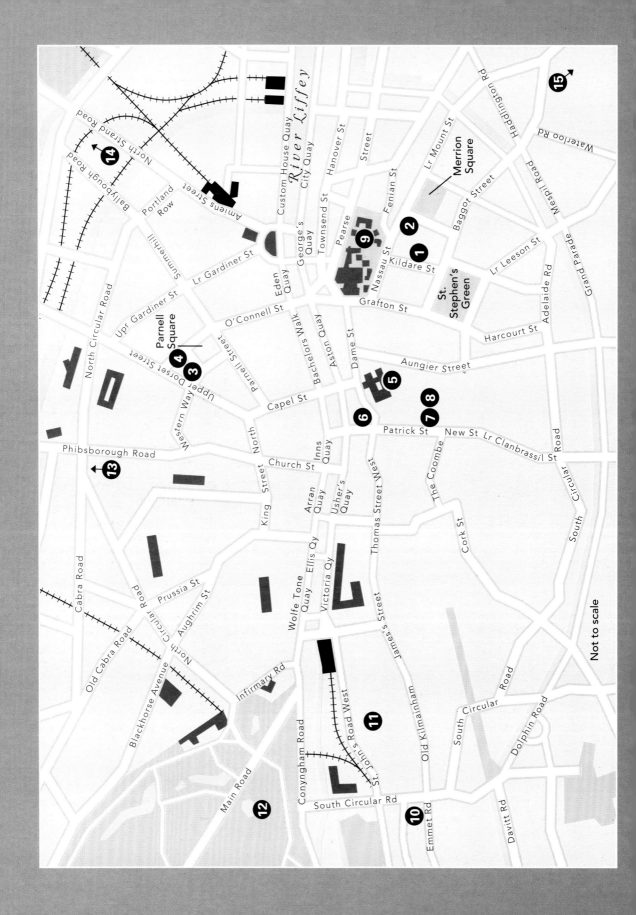

River Liffey

Custom House Quay
City Quay
George's Quay
Townsend St
Hanover St
Pearse Street
Fenian St
Lr Mount St
Merrion Square
Baggot Street
Haddington Rd
Waterloo Rd
Mespil Road
Grand Parade

North Strand Road
Ballybough Road
Portland Row
Amiens Street
Summerhill
Lr Gardiner St
Upr Gardiner St
Parnell Square
Parnell Street
Upper Dorset Street
North Circular Road
O'Connell St
Eden Quay
Bachelors Walk
Aston Quay
Dame St
Grafton St
Nassau St
Kildare St
St. Stephen's Green
Lr Leeson St
Adelaide Rd
Harcourt St

Aungier Street

Western Way
Capel Street
North King Street
Church St
Inns Quay
Arran Quay
Usher's Quay
Thomas Street West
Patrick St
The Coombe
New St
Lr Clanbrassil St
Cork St
South Circular Road

Phibsborough Road

Cabra Road
Old Cabra Road
North Circular Road
Prussia St
Aughrim St
Blackhorse Avenue
Infirmary Rd
Wolfe Tone Quay
Ellis Qy
Victoria Qy
James's Street
St. John's Road West
Conyngham Road
Old Kilmainham
Emmet Rd
Davitt Rd
Dolphin Road
South Circular Road

Main Road
South Circular Rd

Not to scale

1
2
3
4
5
6
7
8
9
10
11
12
13
14
15

1 NATIONAL MUSEUM OF IRELAND

Prehistoric, Bronze-Age and early-Christian artefacts, of which the most famous are the Ardagh Chalice and Tara Brooch, are among the extensive collections. (Open Tue–Sat and Sun afternoon. Phone 01 618811)

2 NATIONAL GALLERY OF IRELAND

Opened in 1864, the gallery houses collections of paintings from all the European schools as well as Irish artists, including Yeats, Lavery, Osborne and Orpen. (Open Mon–Sat and Sun afternoon. Phone 01 615133)

3 HUGH LANE MUNICIPAL GALLERY

The Hugh Lane collection of 19th and 20thC paintings is shared with London's National Gallery. Under the current agreement 30 pictures from the collection are on show. (Open Tue–Sun. Phone 01 741903)

4 DUBLIN WRITERS' MUSEUM

Lively exhibitions trace the Irish literary tradition from the *Book of Kells* to the 20thC, with attention paid to the lives and works of authors including Jonathan Swift, Oscar Wilde, W. B. Yeats, Sean O'Casey, George Bernard Shaw, Brendan Behan and James Joyce. The two Georgian houses which contain the museum also feature a living writers centre, children's bookshop, library of rare volumes, Tara's Palace (a magnificent doll's palace) and a restaurant. (Open Mon–Sat and Sun afternoon. Phone 01 722239)

5 DUBLIN CASTLE

Built at the heart of historic Dublin, the castle gardens are on the site of the black pool ('dubh linn') from which the city gets its name. Today's castle buildings include a diverse collection of architectural styles, ranging from part of the original structure commissioned in the 13thC by King John, to George's Hall, built as a supper room in 1911. The castle was the citadel of English authority in Ireland, serving as a fort, prison, treasury and courts until it was handed over to the provisional Irish Government in 1922. Today, Dublin Castle contains government offices and is used for important State occasions. The State apartments, undercroft and chapel are open to the public. (Open Mon–Fri and Sat and Sun afternoon. Phone 01 777580/777129)

6 CHRIST CHURCH CATHEDRAL

The first cathedral was built of wood in 1038 by Sitric, king of Dublin's Norsemen, for Dunan, first Bishop of Dublin. It was rebuilt in stone by 'Strongbow' in the 12thC and restored in the 19thC. Its crypts were once the site of two taverns going by the names of Paradise and Hell! (Open daily. Phone 01 778099)

7 ST. PATRICK'S CATHEDRAL

Ireland's largest church is built on Dublin's oldest Christian site, where St. Patrick carried out baptisms at an adjacent well. A 5thC church was replaced by the existing building in 1191, and it became the first University of Ireland in 1320. Its most famous dean was satirist Jonathan Swift, who is buried inside. (Open daily. Phone 01 754817)

8 MARSH'S LIBRARY

The fascinating book collection of Archbishop Marsh formed Ireland's first public library when it opened in 1701. The library contains the cages into which readers were locked to prevent them from stealing books. A bindery restores and repairs rare volumes. (Open Mon and Wed–Fri, and Sat morning. Phone 01 543511)

9 TRINITY COLLEGE

Founded in 1592 by Elizabeth I, the college's 40 acre site is still secluded, despite its city centre location. The Long Room in the college library was Europe's largest reading room when built in 1712. It contains the magnificent *Book of Kells*. An audiovisual show on Dublin's history – 'The Dublin Experience' – is open during the summer. (Library: open Mon–Fri and Sat morning. Phone 01 772941)

10 KILMAINHAM JAIL

Opened in 1795, this is now the largest unoccupied jail in Ireland and Britain. Many political prisoners, including Charles Stewart Parnell and Robert Emmett, were jailed here and it was also here that the leaders of the 1916 Easter Rising were executed. Guided tours of the building provide a wealth of historical information. (Open daily June–Sep, and Wed and Sun afternoon Oct–May. Phone 01 535984)

11 ROYAL HOSPITAL KILMAINHAM

Built for the old soldiers of Charles II, it remained a veterans' home until 1927. Later it became the Free State's Garda headquarters. It has now been restored and houses the Irish Museum of Modern Art, as well as hosting exhibitions, concerts, etc. (Open Tue–Sun. Phone 01 718666)

12 PHOENIX PARK

The largest city park in Europe, covering 1750 acres. Amenities include the Zoological Gardens (phone 771425), walks, sports fields, a People's Garden, polo grounds and deer herds. The Irish president's and American ambassador's residences are here. Though beautiful, remote areas of the park are not always safe; do not camp here or walk after dark.

13 NATIONAL BOTANIC GARDENS

Opened in 1795, these pleasant grounds, including rock, rose and herb gardens, contain 20,000 different plant species. The curvilinear glasshouses were designed and built by Richard Turner in the 19thC. (Open daily. Phone 01 377596)

14 THE CASINO

This 18thC Palladian casino in Marino, which was designed for Lord Charlemount by Sir William Chambers, took 15 years to complete and cost a huge £20,000. Note that the roof urns are really chimneys! (Open daily mid June–Sep. Phone 01 331618)

15 CHESTER BEATTY LIBRARY

The library contains one of the finest private collections of Islamic and Oriental manuscripts, including a Babylonian clay tablet dating from 2700 BC. (Open daily Tue–Fri and Sat afternoon. Phone 01 692386)

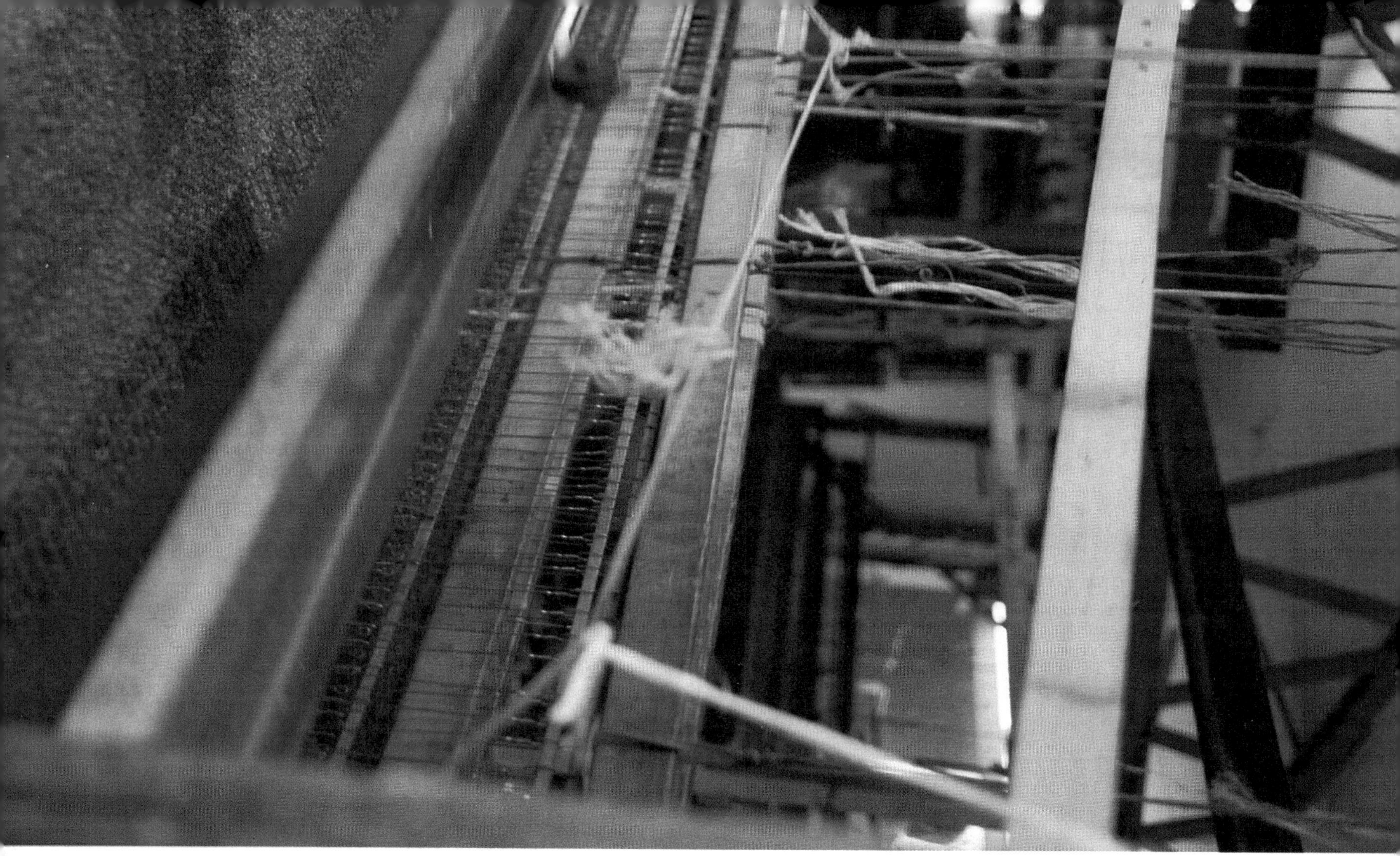

The East

Preceding page: Avoca Handweavers

Above and left: Newgrange Passage Grave, Co. Meath

Beyond the dormitory towns of the region round Dublin lie the rugged Wicklow Mountains, the rich grasslands of counties Meath and Kildare and the great Bog of Allen.

At only 30 miles long, Co. Dublin is an ideal base for touring the east. Just an hour's drive from the city will bring you to the ancient passage grave of Newgrange in Co. Meath, only one of the many prehistoric sites in the fertile Boyne Valley, or into the lovely Vale of Avoca.

Ancient sites are abundant and excavations round Navan have disclosed evidence of human habitation in the Stone Age. The fertile lands of Co. Meath were once part of an ancient fifth province from which the high kings of Ireland ruled from their palace at Tara, and the area known as the Brugh na Boinne complex contains some of Europe's finest prehistoric remains. At the furthest tip of the county are the Loughcrew Mountains, which are covered with a series of ancient cairns dating back almost 5000 years.

Ancient earthworks are also scattered across The Curragh, and the Hill of Allen in northern Co. Kildare was once the winter base for the legendary Fianna warriors.

The region has many historical and religious connections. St. Brigid has many associations with Co. Kildare, while St. Columba founded one of his many monasteries at the village of Moone. Few monastic remains though, can compare with the tranquillity of Glendalough in Co. Wicklow, while Baltinglass's Cistercian abbey was founded on the banks of the Slaney in the 12thC by the king of Leinster, Dermot McMurrough.

At Duleek in Co. Meath, St. Patrick settled St. Cianan to build Ireland's first stone church and

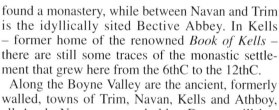

Below: Disused Copper Mine, Avoca, Co. Wicklow   *Above:* The Mottee Stone, Avoca

found a monastery, while between Navan and Trim is the idyllically sited Bective Abbey. In Kells – former home of the renowned *Book of Kells* – there are still some traces of the monastic settlement that grew here from the 6thC to the 12thC.

Along the Boyne Valley are the ancient, formerly walled, towns of Trim, Navan, Kells and Athboy, all Anglo-Norman strongholds. Donore still has its 'Ten Pound Castle', built after Henry VI promised a grant of £10 in 1429 to all his subjects who built a castle 20 ft long, 16 ft wide and 40 ft high within the counties of Meath, Louth, Kildare and Dublin – the area known as the Pale. Trim boasts the remains of the largest Anglo-Norman castle in Ireland among its many medieval attractions; the castle's curtain walls enclose 3 acres. Dunsany Castle, on the slopes of the Hill of Tara, was built in the 12thC to guard the road between Trim and Dublin, and is one of the oldest houses to have been continuously inhabited in Ireland, though only the four towers remain of the original building. (Open Mon–Sat morning, May–mid Aug. Phone 046 31845)

It was in Co. Meath also, at Oldbridge, close to the Co. Louth border, that William II's forces defeated the troops of James I in the Battle of the Boyne, probably the most famous clash in the War of the Kings.

The region is also the location of many 'big houses', due to the high proportion of Norman and English settlers who for centuries controlled the Pale and its rich lands. Among the best known are Kilruddery House, between Bray and Greystones, Russborough House near Blessington and Castletown House in Celbridge.

Co. Meath too, is the site of a modern 'plantation'. Almost 55 years ago families from the Gaeltacht of Connemara were resettled in an area near Athboy, Rath Cairn, by the Land Commission. Today Rath Cairn is a close-knit Gaeltacht community with a growing population, which hosts drama and storytelling festivals, and language courses for both students and adults.

Co. Dublin has a varied coastline, much of it still unspoilt despite the spread of suburbs on both the north and south coasts. Along the coast Dublin leads into Co. Wicklow via Bray, once a Victorian seaside resort, home to James Joyce for three years and now a commuter suburb, and on to the towns of Greystones, Wicklow and Arklow before entering Brittas Bay, a popular seaside destination for Dubliners, and just one of Co. Wicklow's white sandy beaches. North of Dublin are the beaches of Portmarnock, Rush, Skerries, Laytown and Bettystown. Dublin's DART train will take you from Bray to pretty Howth, while ordinary trains run further north and south.

It is the River Liffey which divides north from south in Dublin, and in Co. Kildare the river, spanned by old bridges, once again splits the county's territory, rushing through small villages such as the Viking-settled Leixlip. To the west of Kildare the River Barrow makes up part of the county's boundary as it flows south, and in Athy 16thC White's Castle still guards the bridge which marked a strategic river crossing.

Bypasses, motorways and dual carriageways mean travellers often whiz through Co. Kildare, regarding it only as a gateway to the south or west. Its many historic and elegant towns and villages,

Mount Usher Gardens, Co. Wicklow

Above and below: Howth Harbour, Co. Dublin

The massive peat-covered Wicklow Mountains guard the section of the east coast between Dublin and Wexford. Over a quarter of the land in this county is over 1000 ft above sea level, encompassing some of the wildest and most spectacular scenery in the country. The gorse- and heather-covered hills and peaceful glens are ideal for walkers and cyclists. Beauty spots include the Glen of the Downs, underneath the Sugarloaf, and Glencree. Over 60,000 acres of the county are under forest and it was from Shillelagh – which gave its name to the original cudgels cum walking sticks carried by Irish men – that oak trees were felled to roof both Westminster in London and Dublin's St. Patrick's Cathedral.

Traditionally rebel and bandit country, the mountains were hiding places for many insurgents due to their inaccessibility. It was only after the uprisings of 1798 that the army built a road to patrol the mountains, leading from Rathfarnham in Co. Dublin to Aghavannagh, high in the mountains.

For plant-lovers, Butterstream near Trim in Co. Meath is one of the country's finest gardens, developed by Jim Reynolds over the past two decades. (Phone 046 36017) St. Anne's Park in Raheny has become renowned for its roses, while the lovely Fernhill Gardens are set on a hillside in Sandyford near Stepaside. The Mount Usher Gardens on the banks of the Vartry River in Ashford have over 8 hectares of rare trees and shrubs.

however, warrant a look and include Ballitore, an old Quaker village, Athy, Castledermot, Naas (the county town) and charming Robertstown. Maynooth was built around medieval Maynooth Castle, home to the Fitzgeralds, lords of Kildare for many centuries, and now centred on St. Patrick's College, established as a Catholic seminary in 1521, closed during the Protestant Reformation, and re-opened in 1795. It is now a full university and contains an ecclesiastical museum.

The limestone plains of Co. Kildare make it the breeding ground for some of the greatest horses in the world and it is the site of the National Stud and the Curragh racecourse, the headquarters of Irish racing. Horse-racing has been a regional and national pastime for almost 2000 years.

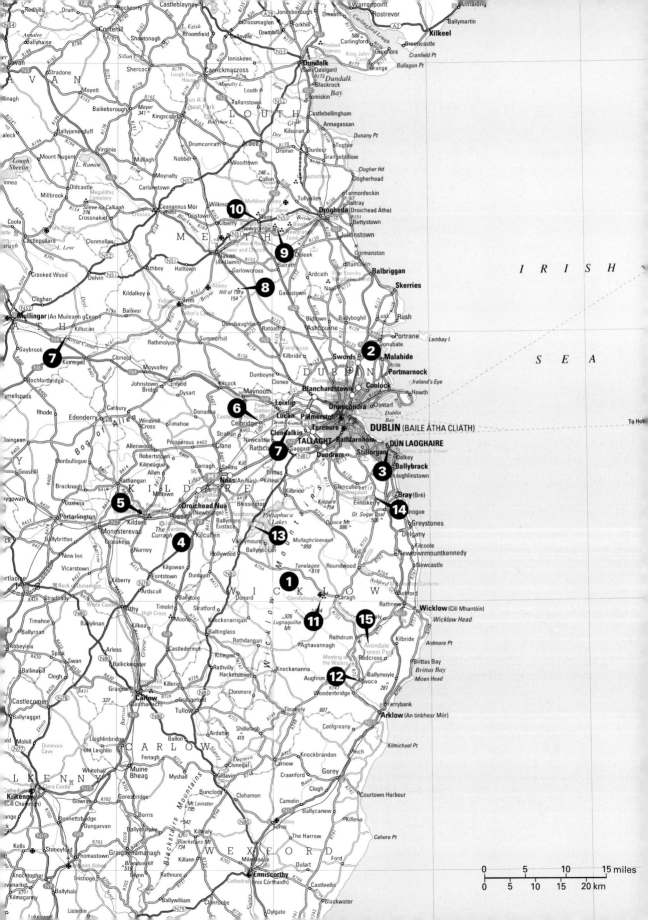

❶ WICKLOW MOUNTAINS

The round-topped hills of counties Dublin and Wicklow make up this national park which includes Ireland's first walking route, the Wicklow Way. Near the beginning of the Way at Marlay Park, Rathfarnham, is the Pearse Museum, once a school run by revolutionary and educationalist Padraic Pearse. (Phone 01 934208) [☙] The highest point, at 3000 ft, is Lugnaquilla; Glencree, Glenmalur and Glenasmole are among the most famous beauty spots.

❷ NORTH DUBLIN VILLAGES

Howth was a 19thC packet station. Its bustling harbour is overlooked by a 13thC parish church. The Howth Castle estate includes a Transport Museum (open daily July–Aug, Sat and Sun, May–June and Sep) [☙], while Howth Head is popular for walks. The demesne of Malahide Castle includes the castle itself, home to the Talbot family for almost 800 years, and the Fry Model Railway Museum. [☙] Portmarnock is famed for both its strand and golf links; both Skerries and Loughshinny have picturesque harbours. Near Donabate is 18thC Newbridge House, designed by Richard Castle for the archbishop of Dublin, with a forge, antique laundry and vinery. (Phone 01 8436534) [☙]

❸ DUN LAOGHAIRE

A popular Victorian resort. Every day hundreds of Dubliners walk the mile-long east pier in the harbour – the west pier is favoured more by anglers. The National Maritime Museum is in the 19thC Mariners' Church. (Phone 01 2800969) There is a museum in the Martello tower in Sandycove where James Joyce stayed briefly and set a chapter of *Ulysses*. (Phone 01 2809265/2808571) Nearby Dalkey has a 16thC town hall and castle. Boat trips operate to Dalkey Island from Coliemore Harbour in summer. Monkstown, home to Culturlann na hEireann, has traditional music.

❹ THE CURRAGH

Ireland's largest area of arable land. Apart from the Curragh racecourse, this 5000 acres is home to sheep, horse studs and the Curragh Camp, an army training centre with a military museum. (Open by appointment)

❺ KILDARE

Kildare has many associations with St. Brigid, Ireland's second saint, who founded a convent where Kildare Cathedral now stands. The National Stud is on the outskirts of the town. (Guided tours available) The adjacent Japanese Gardens plot the life of man. (Phone 045 21251) [☙]

❻ CELBRIDGE

Beautifully located on the Liffey, Celbridge was built as the estate village of Castletown House, built in 1722 and once the largest private house in Ireland. (Phone 01 6288252) Celbridge Abbey was the home of Esther Vanhomrigh, Dean Swift's 'Vanessa'. (Phone 01 6271849)

❼ THE CANALS

The Royal and Grand canals, built in the 18thC, flow into the heart of Ireland. The Grand Canal was used for freight until 1959, and runs from Dublin to Monasterevin, where it crosses the River Barrow on an 18thC viaduct, while the Royal Canal runs towards Mullingar. Barge trips run from the Grand Canal Hotel, Robertstown.

❽ HILL OF TARA

This low hill was the ancient home of the kings of Ireland, a place of religious and political importance for over 2000 years, and stayed in use until 1022. Its remains, though still extensive, are not very spectacular, but development works are planned. (Open daily) [☙]

❾ BRUGH NA BOINNE

This area between Tullyallen and Slane contains about 40 prehistoric sites, said to be evidence of the most advanced Neolithic civilization in Europe. The most famous, the restored Newgrange cairn and tomb, took 18,000 tonnes of stone to build, is over 5000 years old and is said to be the world's first solar observatory. (Visitor centre: open daily) [☙] The nearby burial site of Knowth is 500 years older. Two passage graves in the mound and 18 satellite tombs have been located. Dowth, another chambered burial mound, is currently closed to the public. A medieval church and castle stand nearby.

❿ SLANE

A neat village on a steep hill above the Boyne. Nearby is St. Patrick's Hill, with the remains of a 16thC friary, where the saint is said to have lit the first Paschal fire in AD 433 to announce the arrival of Christianity in Ireland. The 18thC Slane Castle was badly damaged by fire in 1991. On the other side of the village is the restored cottage of war poet Francis Ledwidge, who died in Flanders in 1917. (Open Sat–Thu, summer)

⓫ GLENDALOUGH

Even at its busiest there is a unique tranquillity in Glendalough – 'the valley of the two lakes'. A monastic settlement founded by St. Kevin in the 6thC flourished here for over 600 years, surviving many Viking attacks before being burned and abandoned in 1398. Buildings include a 103 ft round tower, 7thC cathedral and a 12thC monastic cemetery. (Visitor centre: open daily, except Mon, Nov–Mar. Phone 0404 45325) [☙]

⓬ VALE OF AVOCA

A renowned beauty spot. The Meeting of the Waters near Avoca village, where the Avonmore and Avonbeg rivers meet, was made famous by poet Thomas Moore.

⓭ RUSSBOROUGH HOUSE

This 18thC Palladian mansion designed by Richard Castle houses the magnificent Beit Collection of paintings by, among others, Goya, Reubens and Velazquez. There is also fine plasterwork, furniture, carpets and silver. (Open daily July–Aug and Sun and public holiday afternoons Easter–May and Sep–Oct)

⓮ ENNISKERRY

This picturesque hamlet was the estate village of Powerscourt House, gutted by fire in 1974. The 18th and 19thC formal gardens in the adjacent Powerscourt estate, and its nearby waterfall, are a favourite with picnickers. (Open daily)

⓯ AVONDALE

The home of 19thC Nationalist leader, Charles Stewart Parnell. The grounds are now a forest park.

The northern boundaries of the three counties of Cavan, Monaghan and Louth mark the artificial border which divides Ireland in two. There is a somewhat gloomy atmosphere which pervades the northern reaches of these counties. Border towns such as Clones have been economically and socially damaged by the cheaper prices a few miles away in Northern Ireland, and by the closure of roads linking North and South for security reasons.

The Cooley peninsula is one of the few areas, apart from the region's fisheries, frequented by residents from both sides of the border and there is still an unquenchable magic to be found in the landscape and towns.

The area is sprinkled with lakes and small rivers which enticed early settlers and today attract the fishermen. The abundance of Stone-Age tombs and dolmens, of which the most famous is the Proleek Dolmen at Ballymascanlan in Co. Louth, bear evidence that the region has been populated for thousands of years.

Preceding page: Musicians at Carrick-on-Shannon

The small rounded hills that you will see throughout the region, particularly Co. Monaghan, are drumlins, glacial formations up to 100 ft high, and the soft, sheltered landscape they provide drew the early Christians, who founded many monasteries. On a hill in Faughart, Co. Louth, is a shrine to St. Brigid, Ireland's second saint, who was born nearby.

Above and below: Muckno Park, Castleblaney

Below: St. Lawrence's Gate, Drogheda   *Above:* Carrick-on-Shannon

While the Normans came and took over the coasts of Co. Louth, the Irish clans retained power inland until the arrival of Cromwell and then the defeat of James II. Drogheda was the site of 'The Protector's first massacre and later much of the land in the area, particularly the east, was 'planted' with loyal English and Scottish settlers.

It was just south of Drogheda, meanwhile, that the Battle of the Boyne took place at Oldbridge in 1690, when the deposed Catholic king, James II, was defeated by William of Orange. It was the turning point in the War of the Kings.

This is also a land of legends. The beautiful Cooley peninsula is where ancient Ulster's great hero, Cuchulainn, fought the warriors of Maeve, the queen of Connacht, over the Brown Bull of Cooley. The flatlands west of Dundalk are where he is said to have been born, and where he died from battle wounds, strapped to a stone pillar and fighting to the end.

Today it is a slow-moving, rural area. There are no flash tourist amenities or vamped-up villages, but there are still some unexpected modern surprises, such as the magnificent Slieve Russel Hotel, which appears almost like a mirage as you drive from Belturbet towards the Iron Mountains.

Castle Roche, built in the 13thC on a rocky outcrop, is probably the region's most romantic ruin, with its curtained walls and towered gate. It was built as a frontier fort to defend the Pale, the area controlled by the English throughout Leinster.

25

Above and below: Derragarra Inn, Butlers Bridge

Louth is Ireland's smallest county, made up initially of gentle hills and flatlands, before bursting into the spectacular mountainous region around Cooley.

Castlebellingham still has a distinctive olde-worlde flavour, while the courthouse in the small town of Ardee is a 15thC castle, once the largest fortified home in Ireland. At Kildemock near Ardee is the 'Jumping Church'. According to tradition, the 16 ft wall of this ruined church jumped 3 ft inwards in order to keep the grave of an excommunicated Catholic outside its sacred ground!

It is said that Co. Cavan has a lake for every day of the year. Few would argue with the claim, and it is also here that the sources of both the Shannon, which flows south, and the Erne, which flows north, are to be found. Cavan town was the former seat of the O'Reillys, chiefs of East Breifne. The town grew around a Franciscan friary built in 1300 but, following its destruction by the Williamite forces in 1690, nothing now remains. The Cavan Crystal factory on the town's outskirts offers guided tours during the summer, and boat trips operate on the lakes from Belturbet.

Brackley Lough, Co. Cavan

As well as its lakes, sombre northern mountains and farmland, Co. Cavan is made up of small villages and market towns, many founded by the 'planters'. Belturbet, on a hill beside the Erne, is popular for boating and fishing, while Cootehill has a splendid Palladian mansion in Bellamont Forest. Virginia, built as a garrison town in 1610, is now a popular tourist base on the shores of Lough Ramor.

Monaghan is a quiet, neat county of small farmsteads, market towns, crumbling 'big houses' and of course gentle hills, lakes and rivers. Its atmos-

phere is still best invoked by the poetry of Patrick Kavanagh, born at Inishkeen, who wrote much about its 'stoney grey soil' and 'black hills'. Another famous son of Monaghan is John Robert Gregg, who devised Gregg's shorthand in the early 19thC.

Carrickmacross, the county's second town, is famed for its lace-making, while to the west, the market town of Clones still has the remains of a 12thC Augustinian abbey and an early round tower. Ballybay, once a successful linen town, retains many of its 18th and 19thC buildings.

Leprechaun's Suit at Carlingford

Traveller at Dowra

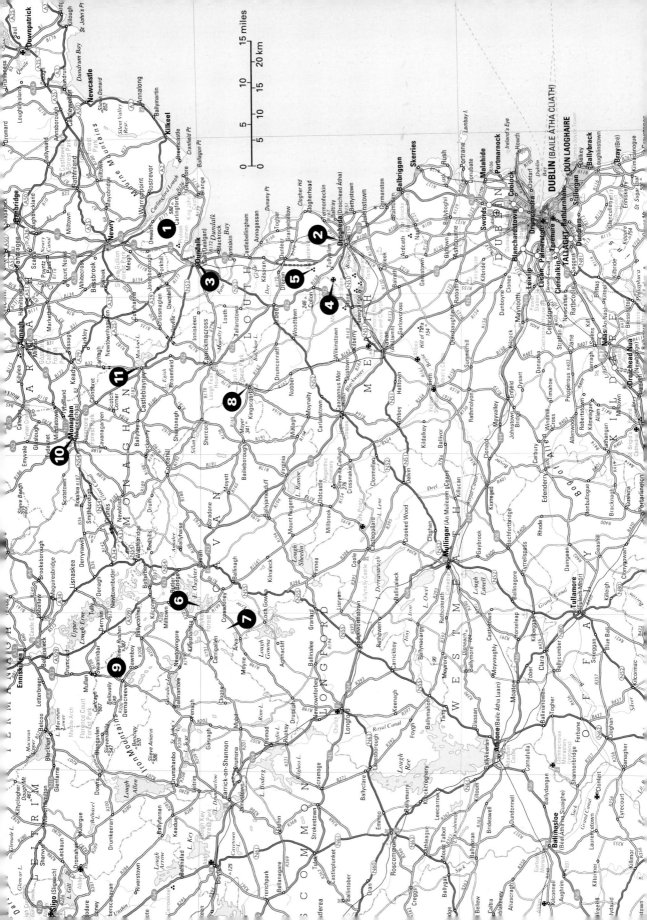

❶ COOLEY PENINSULA

This peninsula, which features prominently in many Irish legends, divides Dundalk Bay from Carlingford Lough and incorporates the Cooley Mountains, with Sliabh Foye rising to 1935 ft. The privately-owned port at the one-street hamlet of Greenore has a Welsh air, while the peace of Carlingford Lough is only disturbed by the sound of British Army helicopters patrolling the border. Carlingford, at the foot of Sliabh Foye, is a good base for those wishing to explore the surrounding hills. The oldest remains are King John's Castle, built by Hugh de Lacy in the 12thC, straddling the main road on the lough edge. The narrow village streets also contain a 15thC mint, and a gatehouse which served as a town hall and 18thC jail. Taafes Castle is a fortified 16thC town house. Ask for directions to the 'magnetic hill' where cars defy gravity, and look out for the Leprechaun suit at O'Hare's Bar.

❷ DROGHEDA

Founded by the Vikings, the town of Drogheda was originally two walled settlements on either side of the Boyne. It became an important English base during medieval times and still retains many old buildings in its 13thC streets. The squat, turret-shaped building on a hill on the Meath side of the town is Mill Mount, a Norman motte built in the 12thC over a prehistoric tomb. It now contains the wonderful museum of the Old Drogheda Society. (Phone 041 33484) Remains of the old walls include St. Lawrence's Gate, with a portcullis, which can be seen at the junction of Palace and St. Lawrence streets. The embalmed head of martyred St. Oliver Plunkett is on view in St. Peter's Church. *i* 041 37070

❸ DUNDALK

Established in the 12thC, the town was an important outpost fortress for the English Pale during the Middle Ages, and a base for English attacks on the Irish chieftains of Ulster. It takes its name – Dun Dealgan – from the Norman motte, which is now overgrown, to the west. According to tradition, this site was once the home of Cuchulainn. Today it is a busy port and its most notable building is the neoclassical courthouse. *i* 042 35484

❹ MELLIFONT ABBEY

Ireland's first Cistercian abbey, founded in 1142. The abbey took 15 years to build and flourished for over 400 years before being suppressed by Henry VIII. Its later history includes its conversion to a mansion by the earl of Drogheda, an attack by Cromwellian troops, its use as the HQ for Williamite forces during the Battle of the Boyne, and in the 19thC its use as a pigsty! Today, little remains of this once magnificent abbey, and only the lavabo, where the monks washed, is anywhere near its original height. (Open daily)

❺ MONASTERBOICE

Founded by St. Buithe in the 5thC, the remains at this early monastic site include two 13thC churches, a round tower, a decorated slab, and the renowned 10thC high crosses with carvings depicting biblical scenes. (Open daily)

❻ KILLYKEEN FOREST PARK

Killykeen in its Irish form – Coill Chaoin – means delightful wood, a very apt description for this beautiful park. The area round Lough Oughter has been populated for thousands of years, and crannogs (lake dwellings) have been found on the islands. Thirteenth-century Cloughoughter Castle, an O'Reilly tower fort, was built over a crannog. Killykeen is a renowned coarse fishing venue. [🐟]

❼ CAVAN FOLK MUSEUM

Off the beaten track, this museum near Cornafean is in a private house. Known as the 'Pig House Collection', its exhibits include costumes, household goods and furniture dating from the 1700s. Only a fraction of this incredible collection has been catalogued to date. (Phone 049 37248)

❽ KINGSCOURT & DUN A'RI

Kingscourt stands in the beautiful forest park of Dun a'Ri on the River Cabra. The stained-glass windows in its Catholic church, the work of Evie Hone, are renowned. The 560 acre park includes the holy well of Tobar na Splinc, a ruined 17thC fortress and an ice house. There is a wishing well located near Cromwell's Bridge and panoramic views from the hilltop.

❾ WEST CAVAN

West Cavan is wilder, higher and more sombre than the rest of the county, with worthwhile drives over the dark slopes of the Iron and Cuilcagh mountains. Ballyconnell is at the centre of plans to build a canal linking the rivers Shannon and Erne. Swanlinbar, once a thriving spa resort, was named after the founders of its former iron mill, Mr Swann, Mr Linn and Mr Barr. Blacklion is the start of the Cavan Way walk, which goes south to Dowra, the first village on the Shannon river, where there is the Worm Ditch or Black Pig's Race, a 3 mile-long earthwork believed to have marked an ancient Ulster border. The walk also passes through Burren Forest, site of many megalithic tombs. The Shannon Pot, the source of the river, is in a field on the southern slopes of the Cuilcagh Mountains. In a field near Moneygashel post office is an old sweathouse, the Irish version of a sauna, which was used until 1923.

❿ MONAGHAN TOWN

For centuries a base of the MacMahon clan, the present town was planned by 17thC English and Scottish settlers and consists of 3 squares linked by lanes. The pretty Market House at the top of Market St was built in 1792 and now houses the tourist office. The award-winning County Museum on nearby Hill St traces the history of Monaghan and includes the magnificent Cross of Clogher, dating from c. 1400, and folklore and craft exhibits. (Open Tue–Sat. Phone 047 82928) A heritage centre at the Convent of the Order of St. Louis tells the story of the Order's history in the area and the revival of lace-making in the county. *i* 047 81122

⓫ CASTLEBLAYNEY

Built by English 'planters', the Blayneys, the history of this settlement in fact dates back to early Christian times. The town's two main streets lead to a fine Georgian courthouse. Magnificent Muckno Park, the demesne of Hope Castle, has boating and coarse fishing facilities on Muckno Lough (Co. Monaghan's largest lake), as well as nature trails and picnic sites. (Open daily. Phone 042 46356)

The Southeast

Preceding page: Dunmore Cave   *Above:* Enniscorthy

Left: Wexford   *Above:* Kilkenny Castle

T his is the first region visitors arriving at the port of Rosslare will see, an area that combines magnificent beaches, gentle coasts and picturesque river valleys with some of the country's finest medieval remains.

The family names of Co. Wexford reflect the distinctly different cultures that existed here: the Irish; the Norsemen; the Norman, Flemish and Welsh soldiers hired in the 12thC by the king of Leinster; and the English settlers and officials of the 16th, 17th and 18thC. Uniquely, there were three spoken languages still in use here until the 19thC: Irish, English and the Yola dialect. Physical remains of these ethnic groups include the windmill at Tacumashane, which uses a technique introduced by the families of Flemish mercenaries.

Thousands of Wexford men continued the seafaring tradition of their Norse ancestors, of which the most famous is Commodore John Barry, founder of the American Navy. Today, many international sailors are familiar with the inland port of steep-streeted New Ross.

Co. Wexford is also the ancestral home of assassinated American president John F. Kennedy. An arboretum, located near New Ross, on the slopes of Slieve Coilte – a hill that rises above the ancestral home of the Kennedys in Dunganstown – is dedicated to the president.

The southeast of Co. Wexford has record hours of sunshine for Ireland, which is why thousands of Dubliners spend their summer holidays at the resorts and beaches which stretch for 30 miles from east of Gorey to Curracloe, just north of Wexford town. The little inland villages along the coast, such as Ballygarret, Kilmuckridge and Blackwater, with its famous ducks, also have a quiet attraction. Further from the coast, Mount Leinster rises over the attractive town of Bunclody, and the ruins of Ferns' castle and cathedral still survey their former domain.

St. Canice's Cathedral, Kilkenny

Waterford Crystal

Waterford has been part of both Leinster and Munster, eventually settling for the latter province. Waterford Harbour, where the Three Sisters, the rivers Barrow, Nore and Suir, enter the sea, provided a gateway into southern Ireland for many invaders, including the Norsemen. And when Dermot McMurrough invited the Anglo-Normans to help him in his struggle against rival kings, it was through Waterford that 'Strongbow's armies came.

The greatest invasion these days occurs every summer when hundreds of schoolchildren attend colleges in the Gaeltacht area of Ring. Here, the Irish language has survived as the first tongue in an isolated pocket of land around the lovely Helvick Head.

Indented by the estuaries of the rivers Slaney, Barrow, Suir and Blackwater, the coastline of counties Wexford and Waterford is broken up into a succession of beaches, rocky peninsulas and grassy headlands. To the north the landscape begins to open out, and behind the pretty Waterford coast gently rolling pastures stretch back to the slopes of the Knockmealdown, Monavullagh and Comeragh mountain ranges, where the lovely Lough Coumshingaun is partially encircled by 1300 ft glacial cliffs.

Above: Kells Priory, Co. Kilkenny

Below: Dunmore Cave, Co. Kilkenny

The inland area of counties Carlow and Kilkenny consists of a patchwork of pastures and fields sheltered by hills and mountains, and split by the rivers Barrow, Nore and Slaney. The countryside around Co. Carlow is a mass of woods, fields, hedgerows, and scores of pretty villages such as St. Mullins and Leighlinbridge.

Like many other parts of Ireland, local history in Carlow is a melange of eras and events. The history of 17thC Huntingdon Castle near Clonegal includes not only associations with monks, Ann Boleyn and Cromwell, but also the Egyptian goddess Isis. The castle owner, Lawrence Durdin-Robertson, founded the Fellowship of Isis here in 1976 and there are shrines in the castle cellars.

Carlow town itself surrounds the walls of a massive Norman castle built to guard an important crossing on the River Barrow. The castle was repeatedly attacked and besieged but was only finally ruined in the 19thC when a local doctor who wanted to turn it into a mental asylum, blew it up when attempting to enlarge the windows using gunpowder! The building which houses the town library was donated by George Bernard Shaw, while a museum at the rear of the town hall

Above: Country Lane near Kells

Below: Rothe House, Kilkenny

contains some interesting local curios, including the old public gallows.

Kilkenny, though only a town in size, has the status of a city. It vied with Dublin for the position of capital during the 17thC and today is one of Ireland's most attractive towns or cities, containing an absolute treasury of well-preserved medieval buildings. Famous citizens include Dame Alice Kytler, a 14thC moneylender who was charged with witchcraft and of poisoning her four husbands. She escaped to Scotland but her maid was burnt at the stake.

The dominant family in the region for many centuries were the Butlers, earls of Ormond, who ruled for about 550 years from their castle in Kilkenny city. Their great rivals were the Fitzgeralds of Munster, earls of Desmond. The two families, however, joined forces in 1642. With other ruling Irish families they formed the Confederation of Kilkenny to fight against the domination of Protestant England. In retaliation for their actions, many of them lost their lands to Protestants who were 'planted' by the Crown. The tradition of insurrection remained strong in the southeast, however, particularly around Wexford, where the main thrust of the 1798 rebellion of the United Irishmen against English rule took place.

Of a more peaceful disposition were the monks who chose some of the region's finest beauty spots, such as Ardmore in Co. Waterford and Graiguenamanagh ('dwelling of the monks') in Co. Kilkenny. Our Lady's Island, in a salt lake near Carnsore, is the site of one of the oldest pilgrimages in Ireland. The causeway connecting it to the mainland is believed to have been built by pre-Norman monks.

Scenic drives in the region include the Comeragh and Nire Valley drives in west Waterford, and the Knockmealdown Drive which leads from near Lismore to the spectacular Vee into south Tipperary.

The River Barrow is navigable and cruisers from the Grand Canal come as far south as St. Mullins. Another delightful way to see the countryside is by taking a tour on a Galley Cruising Restaurant along the Barrow, Nore or Suir. Departures are from New Ross and Waterford city. (Phone 051 21723)

Reginald's Tower, Waterford

Above: Jerpoint Abbey, Co. Kilkenny   *Below:* Rosemount Stud, Inistioge   *Above:* Thomastown   *Below:* Inistioge

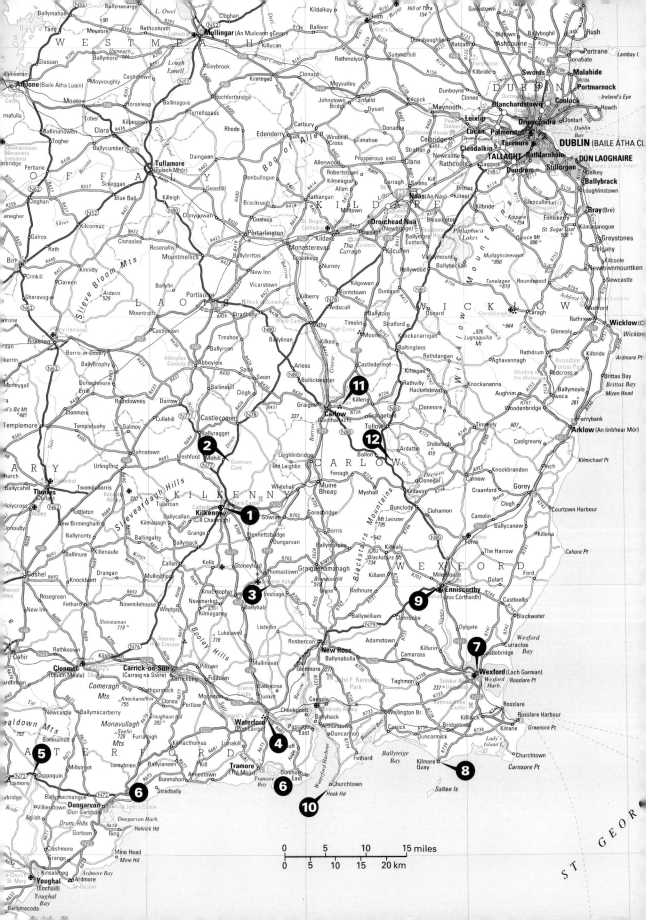

❶ KILKENNY CITY

The Shee Almshouse, built in 1528 by lawyer Sir Robert Shee for 12 paupers, is now the tourist office. Twelfth-century Kilkenny Castle, overlooking the Nore, was the seat of the Butler family. (Open Tue–Sun, Mar, Oct and Nov, daily April–Sep. Phone 056 21450) Rothe House, a Tudor merchant's house, is now a museum. (Phone 056 22893) St. Canice's Cathedral, completed in 1285, is still in use. It is also possible to climb the adjacent round tower, built 300 years earlier on the 6thC monastic site founded by St. Canice. (Open daily) The Black Abbey, a Dominican friary founded in 1225, has been restored, while the remains of another 13thC abbey have been preserved off Parliament St at St. Francis' Abbey Brewery, founded in 1710. (Guided tours Mon–Fri, June–Sep. Phone 056 21014) *i* 056 21755

❷ DUNMORE CAVE

The spectacular formations of these ancient limestone caves include the 20 ft-wide Market Cross. (Open Tue–Sat and Sun afternoon, mid Mar–mid June, daily, mid June–mid Sep, Sat, Sun and public holidays, mid Sep–mid Mar) [symbol]

❸ NORE VALLEY

At Kells monks surrounded their priory with a curtain wall as protection. The remains of Jerpoint Abbey, a 12thC Cistercian abbey, are near Thomastown. (Open Tue–Sat and Sun afternoon, May–mid June, daily mid June–mid Sep) Thomastown is a former walled medieval settlement. At Inistioge a Norman motte overlooks the river, and the nearby Woodstock estate contains the ruins of two castles.

❹ WATERFORD CITY

The busy port of Waterford, founded by the Norsemen, is best known for its crystal. Visitors are welcome at the Waterford Crystal factory's centre in Kilbarry. (Showrooms and video presentation: open Mon–Fri and Sat morning. Guided tours. Phone 051 73311) The city's most historic building is Reginald's Tower. Built in 1003 by the Normans, it now houses the city's museum. (Open Mon–Fri and Sat morning, May–Sep) A her-

itage centre is housed in an old Methodist church in Greyfriars St near the ruined French Church, founded by the Franciscans in the 13thC and handed over to a colony of French Huguenot refugees in 1693. Other ecclesiastical sites include Blackfriar's Abbey, one of the country's oldest Dominican foundations, and 9thC St. Olave's Church. The Protestant Christ Church Cathedral and Catholic Holy Trinity Cathedral are also worth a visit. Walking tours of the city leave in summer from the tourist information office on The Quay. *i* 051 75823

❺ BLACKWATER VALLEY

Cappoquin, where the Blackwater and Glenshelane rivers meet, stands at the foot of the Knockmealdown Mountains. Cappoquin House was rebuilt after a fire in 1923 but reversed so its occupants could enjoy views of the river. (Open mornings, April–July. Phone 058 54004) The grounds of Lismore Castle, Irish seat of the earl of Devonshire, are open on summer afternoons.

❻ COASTAL WATERFORD

From Passage East, at the bottom of steep cliffs, a ferry service operates to Ballyhack in Co. Wexford. Dunmore East, a former mail packet station, is now a charming fishing and sailing village. Tramore is a busy seaside resort. Celtworld, a three-dimensional audiovisual show, depicts the legends and mythical heroes of Ireland. (Open daily) [symbol] At the handsome port of Dungarvan are the ruins of a 12thC castle. An Rinn (Ring) is part of the Deise Gaeltacht, and the seaside village of Ardmore is overlooked by one of Ireland's finest round towers.

❼ WEXFORD TOWN

This bustling town owes its narrow streets and name – Weissfjord – to the Vikings. The town hosts a world-famous Opera Festival in late Oct/early Nov. The huge Westgate at the top of Slaney St is the only surviving gateway of the town's walls. At Ferrycarraig, to the east of the town, is the outstanding National Irish Heritage Park, with full-size replicas of buildings and burial places dating from up to the 12thC. (Open daily, April–Oct) [symbol] Northeast of the town are the North Sloblands, a

300 acre bird reserve, while a few miles south is Johnstown Castle, an agricultural research centre and museum in ornamental grounds. (Gardens: open daily. Museum: open Mon–Fri and Sat and Sun afternoon, April–mid Nov) [symbol]

❽ KILMORE QUAY

A picturesque fishing village with whitewashed thatched cottages. A seafood festival in July includes a trawler race round the Saltee Islands. The lightship *Guillemot* berthed in the harbour is now a maritime museum. (Open daily, June–Sep) [symbol]

❾ ENNISCORTHY

A settlement founded by St. Senan in AD 510. In 1205 the Normans built a castle overlooking the River Slaney. Over the centuries its occupants included the poet Edmund Spenser, and today the castle contains the county museum. (Open Mon–Sat and Sun afternoon, June–Sep, afternoons Feb–May and Oct) One of Ireland's most famous battles was fought here on Vinegar Hill during the 1798 Rebellion. The town hosts a Strawberry Festival in early July.

❿ HOOK HEAD

The ship beacon at this point was first attended by Welsh missionary Dubhan (Dubhan means 'hook'). There are monastic cells set into the base of the current tower, part of a Norman structure said to be Europe's first lighthouse. The Ring of Hook drive goes through the resort of Fethard-on-Sea, an ancient seafaring settlement. Slade is a fishing harbour with the remains of a castle and salt houses. A little north of the peninsula is 12thC Tintern Abbey.

⓫ BROWN'S HILL DOLMEN

On the Hacketstown road outside Carlow town, this megalithic monument dates from c. 2000 BC. Its capstone weighs about 100 tons and is said to be the largest in Europe.

⓬ ALTAMONT GARDENS

The grounds along the River Slaney include formal gardens, a nuns' walk, and a lake dug during the Famine years to give employment. (Open Sun afternoon. Phone 053 57128)

Preceding page: The Blasket Islands *Above:* Ring of Kerry

So mahy of Ireland's greatest beauty spots are concentrated in the two counties of Cork and Kerry that it is no surprise they have attracted hordes of visitors since the mid-1700s. Yet few places in this region are ever overcrowded, apart from some of the glories which surround Killarney and its lakes.

It is thought that because of its proximity to Europe, Christianity may have reached the southwest before even St. Patrick. The Anglo-Normans also recognized the ease of access between the southwest and Continental Europe, building fortresses and towers across both counties. But the Europeans still came. In 1601 the Spanish helped the O'Donnell and O'Neill chieftains take a final stand against English rule – they were defeated at the Battle of Kinsale. Almost 200 years later a French fleet, which carried Irish rebel Wolfe Tone, was forced back only by ferocious storms when it arrived in Bantry Bay to assist the United Irishmen in the 1798 Rebellion. French ships also attacked Bantry in 1689 in a gesture of support for the ousted James II. There were frequent other attacks. Baltimore was even raided by Algerian pirates in 1631 and 200 of its inhabitants taken as slaves. In 1916 revolutionary leader Roger Casement was landed at Banna Strand in Co. Kerry with two colleagues by a German submarine but was quickly captured.

Among the great families of this region were the MacCarthys, who built strongholds across their lands. The town square in Macroom is dominated by the entrance to Macroom Castle, virtually all that remains of the 15thC stronghold of the MacCarthys of Muskerry.

Almost everywhere are the remains of ancient and medieval church settlements. The small village of Ardfert in Kerry was once the county's ecclesiastical capital, and it was here that St. Brendan the Navigator was educated by missionaries and later founded a monastery. It was from below Mount Brandon on the Dingle peninsula that he is believed to have set sail with his monastic brothers on the journey that led him to America long before Columbus.

Some of the country's richest grasslands are in the Golden Vale which makes up part of north Cork, and a huge dairy-processing industry operates from Mitchelstown at the foot of the Galtee Mountains. Other towns in the vale include Fermoy on the River Blackwater and Glanworth, site of Ireland's oldest stone bridge. Near Glanworth is the Hag's Bed, or Labbacallee Cairn, a 3500-year-old wedge tomb.

University College Cork

Fungi the Dolphin, Dingle Bay

Gallarus Oratory, Dingle Peninsula

Dingle Harbour, Co. Kerry

East Cork is very much underestimated, though it offers plenty for visitors. Youghal, once a walled port, still contains some medieval architecture, and it was here that Sir Walter Raleigh is said to have been mayor for a short time. He lived at Myrtle Grove, where it is believed he grew Ireland's first potato. East Cork is also the home of Irish whiskey, and the Jameson Heritage Centre at Midleton traces the spirit's history. The harbour at Ballycotton is almost always packed with colourful craft, while inland a round tower rises above the ancient village of Cloyne. Ballymaloe House, off the Ballycotton–Cloyne road, is one of Ireland's most renowned restaurants.

It is to west Cork, however, that most visitors come, attracted by its remote beauty and the charm of its small villages. One west Cork phenomenon is its 'blow-ins', mainly German and Dutch nationals, who moved here in search of an 'alternative' life style.

Among its more accessible villages are Timoleague, which is dominated by the extensive 43

Fota Wildlife Park, near Cobh, Co. Cork

ruins of a 14thC Franciscan friary, peaceful Courtmachsherry, and Clonakilty, a lively summer destination which hosts an international busking festival. Ballinspittle is where two local women claimed to have seen a statue of the Blessed Virgin move, sparking pilgrimages by thousands of people and a spate of moving statues nationwide during the 1980s.

The coastline from Rosscarbery to Baltimore is known as the Yachtsmen's Coast. It was at the steep-streeted village of Castletownshend that Edith Somerville and Violet Martin – Somerville and Ross – wrote their stories of an Irish RM, while the mystical Drombeg Stone Circle is only a couple of miles from the pretty twin villages of Unionhall and Glandore. Skibbereen has a thriving community of artists, craftworkers and musicians, many of them 'blow-ins', and the ancient harbour

Eightercua Stone Alignment, near Waterville, Co. Kerry

village of Baltimore is the embarkation point for Sherkin Island and Cape Clear, both popular summer destinations. Among the region's other islands are the Blaskets, uninhabited since 1953, except Inishvickillane, holiday home of the former Irish Taoiseach (prime minister) Charles Haughey.

Lough Hyne, between Skibbereen and Baltimore, is a landlocked salt lake containing many tropical fish brought into Irish waters by the Gulf Stream. The warmth of the stream also brings other unexpected pleasures, nurturing Mediterranean and even subtropical flowers. Soft warm rain falls throughout the year resulting in a lush vegetation, and Kerry is particularly populated with wild flowers from other climates. Among the region's gardens and parks are Glanleam, where an avenue is lined with tropical tree ferns; Anne's Grove,

Above: Blarney Castle   *Below:* Blennerville Windmill

The Connor Pass, Dingle Peninsula

Dingle

Smoked Salmon, Cork Market

Above: Killarney

Below: Torc Waterfall, near Killarney

Above: Cork   *Below:* Rossbeigh Strand, Co. Kerry

Above and below: Muckross House, near Killarney

near charming Castletownroche; and the wildlife sanctuary at Doneraile Court.

Moving past the Iveragh and Dingle peninsulas towards Limerick and the Shannon estuary, the coast of northwest Kerry consists of long golden beaches, sandy dunes, high cliffs, coves and sea caves. Ballyheigue, with views of the Dingle peninsula, is dominated by the almost Hollywood-style façade of a 19thC castle. Nearby Kerry Head still has the remains of two 2000-year-old forts, underground chambers and beehive houses.

Ballybunion is a popular resort where there's even a chance to enjoy a hot seaweed bath. South of Ballyduff is Rattoo, home to a complete round tower and a heritage museum which illustrates much of north Kerry's intriguing history. (Phone 066 31000) To the north of the little village of Ballylongford are the ruins of Lislaughtin Abbey, built in 1478, and to its west are the remains of Carrigafoyle Castle, which was once the seat of the O'Connors of Kerry. Inland, the busy town of Listowel is famed for its horse races and its Writers Week.

Long-time competitors in the beauty stakes, counties Kerry and Cork are also sporting rivals, particularly on the Gaelic football field. Sport has always been an important feature of life in the southwest and it has historic links with many diverse sporting activities. The first yacht club in Ireland or Britain was at Cobh, while the first steeplechase was run from Buttevant in north Cork in 1752, when riders raced from the church to Doneraile 5 miles away, using the steeple of Doneraile church as their guide. Road bowls or 'bullets' is now only played in the counties of Armagh and parts of Cork, particularly Bantry. The sport entails 'lofting' a 28 oz ball round bends in the road! 47

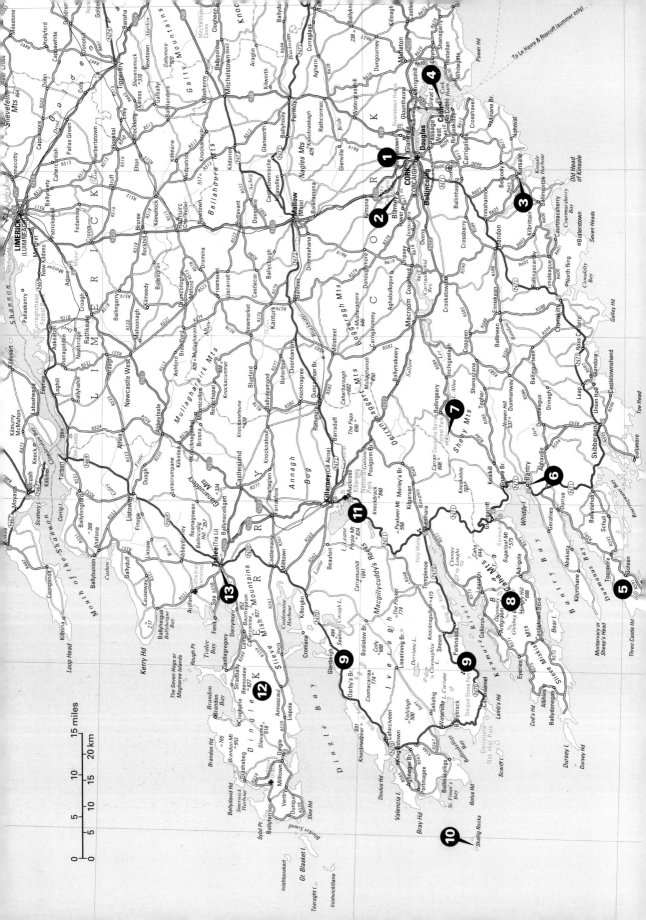

❶ CORK CITY

The 19thC cathedral of St. Finbarr stands on the site where the 7thC saint established a school. Formerly one of Europe's most important ports, many of the main streets were built over boat channels. Visitors can ring the Shandon Bells in St. Anne's Church on the city's north side (open Mon–Sat), and Cork City Museum is in Fitzgerald Park (open Mon–Fri and Sun afternoon). Cork is a lively city, with pubs, galleries and markets. Dunkathel in Glanmire, a late-18thC mansion overlooking the Lee, and nearby Riverstown House, are worthwhile stops. (Open Thu–Sat afternoons, May–Aug) *i* 021 23251

❷ BLARNEY CASTLE

Fifteenth-century Blarney Castle, built by Dermot MacCarthy, king of Munster, has walls 18 ft thick. The Blarney Stone, set in the 83 ft-high battlements, is said to bestow the gift of eloquence on those who kiss it – but it's no easy task. (Open daily) [☙]

❸ KINSALE

This historic town is renowned for its restaurants and yachting facilities. Desmond Castle, or the French Prison, was first used in the 15thC as a customs house. The Old Courthouse is now a museum. The restored Gift Houses were built in 1682 as almshouses and are still in use. Outside the town is Charles Fort, a late-17thC 'star' fort. Kinsale was the HQ for James II's bid to recover the English Crown. *i* 021 772234

❹ COBH

This resort's harbour was used by 19thC emigrant ships. The port was also a stopping point for transatlantic liners, including the *Titanic* on her only voyage. Many victims of the *Lusitania* are buried in the town, and the maritime museum includes a display on the disaster.

❺ MIZEN HEAD PENINSULA

Ireland's most southerly point. Ballydehob has a flourishing artistic community while Schull, with Ireland's only planetarium, is popular for yachting. The peninsula's best-known beaches are at Barleycove.

❻ BANTRY

This market town and fishing port has a beautiful location at the head of Bantry Bay. Its museum is full of historical knick-knacks. Fascinating Bantry House, built c. 1750, is the seat of the earls of Bantry. (Open daily. Phone 027 50047) *i* 027 50229

❼ GOUGANE BARRA

This beautiful national park covers 1000 acres of spectacular drives, walks and nature trails. It was on the tiny island in Gougane Barra lake that St. Finbarr founded a monastery before moving downriver to Cork.

❽ BEARA PENINSULA

The Caha Mountains form the spine of this rugged peninsula. Drive through Killaha to the Healy Pass and round glorious Inchiquin Lough. The gardens of the Derreen estate are near Lauragh. Glengarriff is usually ablaze with subtropical plant life. Offshore is Garinish Island, an exotic garden created by Scottish MP Annan Bryce and his wife in the 1920s; boats leave from the village. Castletown Bere was used as a British Navy anchorage until 1937. Dursey Island is linked to the peninsula by cable car.

❾ RING OF KERRY

The traditional name for the scenic road round the coast of the Iveragh peninsula. In colourful Kenmare a stone circle stands on the banks of the River Finnighy. Many subtropical plants flourish at Parknasilla. Sneem's pastel-painted cottages have a spectacular location on the estuary of the Sneem river. Staigue Fort, one of Ireland's best-preserved ring forts, is near Castlecove, and near Caherdaniel is Derrynane House, the home of Daniel O'Connell, a great 19thC figure who achieved Catholic emancipation. (Open daily) The fishing and golf are renowned in Waterville. Ballinskelligs is a scenic Gaeltacht village with a 4 mile beach. Valentia Island is popular with anglers and walkers, and Killorglin has the Puck Fair, when a goat is crowned king for three days.

❿ THE SKELLIGS

These massive rocks off the Kerry coast are Little Skellig, a bird sanctu-

ary, and Skellig Michael. Boat trips to the latter leave from Ballinskelligs and Portmagee. Steps in the rock face lead up to a ruined abbey, beehive huts and two oratories. Though plundered by Vikings, the monastery continued until the 12thC.

⓫ LAKES OF KILLARNEY

Three magical lakes at the wooded feet of the highest mountains in Ireland, Macgillycuddy's Reeks. Killarney is well-equipped for tourists. The entrance to Knockreer estate can be found opposite St. Mary's Cathedral. There are boat excursions on Lough Leane. Ask the boatman to take you to Inishfallen Island and O'Sullivan's Cascade. From Kate Kearney's cottage near Beaufort, the magnificent 6 mile Gap of Dunloe passes between the Reeks and Purple Mountain to Lord Brandon's Cottage beside the Upper Lake. The Muckross estate, on Muckross Lake, has a ruined 15thC abbey and Elizabethan-style mansion. The rhododendron-filled grounds have scenic walks and one of the area's loveliest spots, the Meeting of the Waters. (Open daily)

⓬ DINGLE PENINSULA

Dingle is famous as the location for the film *Ryan's Daughter*, its restaurants and Fungi the dolphin. The spectacular Connor Pass begins just outside the town and crosses the Brandon Mountains. Ventry overlooks a superb beach. Further west near Fahan is the Iron-Age fort of Dunbeg, and hundreds of tiny beehive huts (clochans). Slea Head towers above the sea in the shadow of Mount Eagle, and nearby Ballyferriter has a small heritage centre. Also close by is the tiny 9thC Gallarus Oratory.

⓭ TRALEE

Kerry's county town is best known for its Rose of Tralee Festival, held every Aug. In the 16th and 17thC it was the main seat of the earls of Desmond, the Geraldines. An exhibition about Geraldine Tralee is housed in the Ashe Memorial Hall. [☙] Nearby is Blennerville windmill. A narrow-gauge railway runs from the town to the mill during the summer. [☙] Near Castleisland is spectacular Crag Cave. (Open daily, mid Mar–Dec. Phone 066 41244) [☙]

Preceding page: Cliffs of Moher

Rock of Cashel, Co. Tipperary

As the Shannon flows to the sea it marks the borders of the three Munster counties of Limerick, Clare and Tipperary, where the barren hills and jagged coastline of north and west Clare are almost a stark relief after miles of lush green pastures and river valleys.

All three counties, however, boast a similar wealth of historic remains, testimony that for thousands of years this has been a land favoured for habitation by many peoples. Even the bleak Burren was well settled during the Stone and Bronze ages.

Two tribes, the McNamaras and the O'Briens, battled for supremacy here for many centuries, and the centre of power was Cashel in Co. Tipperary. It was near Killaloe, at Kincora, that the founder of the O'Brien clan – and one of the greatest Irish high kings – Brian Boru, had his palace in the 10thC. These two families are responsible for the majority of castles and tower houses which still dominate hundreds of strategic sites.

The only city in the region is Limerick, which, like other Munster settlements, was founded by the Norsemen and developed by the Normans. The Norsemen made their base on an island in the Shannon, from which they marauded through Munster until their defeat in AD 967. The kings of Thomond, the name given to this northern area of the province, then used it as a trading centre. The

Celtic Artefacts, Hunt Museum, Limerick

Anglo-Normans made it an early target, storming it in 1175, but it was recaptured by Donal Mor O'Brien. The town's first charter was bestowed in 1197 and it served as a prosperous English trading colony until it was besieged for 12 months and fell to Cromwell in 1651. In 1690 the town was unsuccessfully attacked and besieged by William of Orange, but another siege in 1691 by General Ginkel brought surrender, under the conditions of a treaty (later ignored) which guaranteed the city's Catholics civil rights and allowed the troops who

Swiss Cottage, Cahir, Co. Tipperary

had been loyal to King James to join the French Army. This departure of 10,000 troops began a massive exodus which became known as the Flight of the Wild Geese.

Early Christianity also marked the foundation of many monasteries in this region and the tradition continued for many centuries, with some of the Cistercian's most famous abbeys, including Holy Cross near Thurles, being built here in the 12thC.

For many visitors the boundary of Limerick and Clare is their first glimpse of Ireland, as the aeroplane swings in across the estuary of the great Shannon river to land at the international airport, which has taken its name from the country's largest river.

Shannon was the first duty-free airport in the world, but the region first made aviation history in the 1930s when Foynes served as the European airbase for the shortlived career of the luxury transatlantic flying boats. The first flight to Newfoundland was made in 1937 and the last in October 1945. There's an aviation museum at Foynes. (Open daily Mar–Oct. Phone 069 65416)

Southwest of Limerick city, a mile-long nature trail leads around a lake, in just part of the superb 600 acre Curraghchase Park, while southeast the Galtee and Ballyhoura mountains slope down to the green plains around medieval Kilmallock, Galbally and the Golden Vale. Bruree village con-tains a museum dedicated to former Taoiseach (prime minister) and president of the Republic, Eamon de Valera, author of the nation's Constitution. Further west again, in the secluded village of Drumcollogher, is the Plunkett Heritage Museum, dedicated to Henry Plunkett, the father of the Irish cooperative movement, who founded a creamery coop here in 1889.

The Burren, Co. Clare

Above: Knappogue Castle, Co. Clare

Below: Castle Matrix, Rathkeale, Co. Limerick

Glin Castle

The Brendan, Craggaunowen Bronze Age Project, Co. Clare

Glin Castle Gardens

East Clare history is recalled in the heritage centres at Tuamgraney and Corofin, both housed in former Protestant churches. And at Dysart O'Dea, south of Corofin, is an award-winning archaeological centre and trail which includes a 15thC castle, 11thC round tower, 7thC monastery and holy wells.

Below The Burren and the Cliffs of Moher is Co. Clare's softer face, including resorts like Lahinch, Milltown Malbay and Spanish Point.

As the Shannon estuary opens to the sea, its shores back on to flatlands bordered by dramatic cliffs rising up from the Atlantic. Kilkee, north of Loop Head, has been a busy seaside resort since the 19thC. It has a wonderful beach and breathtaking cliff walks. The heritage centre at nearby Kilrush focuses particularly on Scattery Island, inhabited until the 1970s, where St. Senan founded a 6thC monastery. Its round tower, with a unique ground-level door, is said to be Ireland's oldest and tallest. Boats leave from nearby Cappagh Pier.

Co. Tipperary's largest town is elegant Clonmel,

situated beside the banks of the River Suir and overlooked by the Comeragh and Knockmealdown mountains. A section of the old town wall surrounds St. Mary's Cathedral, and the old West Gate and Main Guard still loom over the Main St. Ireland's first public transport system, the Bianconi cars founded by mayor Charles Bianconi, began operation here in 1815, running between Cahir and the town.

The manor house in Carrick-on-Suir is one of the region's Tudor buildings. The remains of 15thC Carrick Castle, where Ann Boleyn is reputed to have been born, are fronted by a 16thC manor house built by 'Black Tom', earl of Ormond, in anticipation of a visit from Elizabeth I.

The tower of a Norman castle rises up above busy Nenagh, while Roscrea's heritage centre is in the Queen Anne-style Damer House, built in the courtyard of a massive 13thC castle surrounded by a daunting tower gate and curtain walls.

The region, particularly Co. Clare, is also celebrated for its musicians, and it should not prove hard to find a 'session'. The seaside town of Milltown Malbay comes alive every July for the Willie Clancy Summer School, while the pubs in Ennis, Liscannor, Ennistymon and Doolin resound with song throughout the year. Doolin, also known as Fisherstreet, offers a boat service to the Aran Islands when it's time to move on to the West, or the car ferry service at Killimer will take you to Tarbert in north Kerry.

Ennis Friary, Co. Clare

Lisdoonvarna Spa, Co. Clare
Left: Locke's Bar, Limerick

57

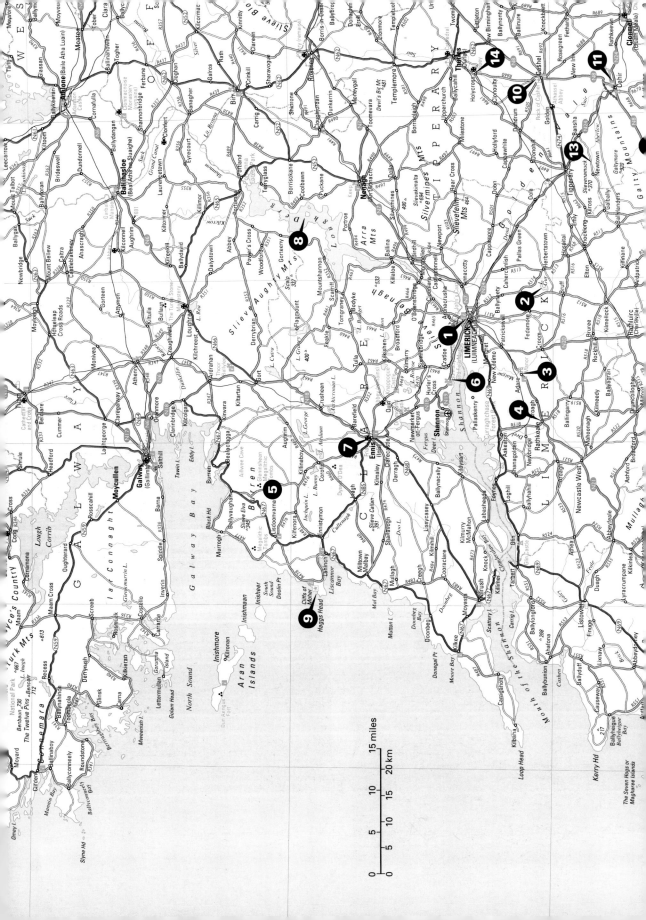

❶ LIMERICK CITY

A 45 min show with spectacular lighting at St. Mary's Cathedral outlines the city's history. (Mid June–mid Sep) King John's Castle, beside Thomond Bridge, has recently been renovated. Displays at the Limerick Museum include Viking artefacts. (Open Tue–Sat) The Hunt Museum at the University of Limerick in Castletroy contains the finest collection of Celtic and medieval treasures outside Dublin's National Museum. On the Bunratty road is Cratloe House, one of the few examples of the Irish longhouse still with a roof. (Open Mon–Sat, June–mid Sep) *i* 061 317522

❷ LOUGH GUR

One of Ireland's most important archaeological sites, with crannogs, stone circles and a gallery grave dated to 2000 BC. Guided tours. (Open daily, May–Sep. Phone 061 85186)

❸ ADARE

This pretty town has a distinctly English character. The 12thC Augustinian abbey is now the local Church of Ireland, while the grander Trinitarian priory is used by the Catholic community. The picturesque thatched cottages were built by the 3rd earl of Dunraven in the 19thC. *i* 061 86255

❹ CASTLE MATRIX

This restored 15thC tower house in Rathkeale takes its name from the Celtic sanctuary of Matres, goddess of love and poetry, on which it stands. It was here that Edmund Spenser and Walter Raleigh met for the first time. It is currently the HQ of the Heraldry Society of Ireland. (Open Sat–Tue, mid May–mid Sep. Phone 069 64284)

❺ THE BURREN

This vast area of limestone slabs, estimated to be over 300 million years old, extends for about 50 miles from Lisdoonvarna towards Galway Bay. Despite its barren appearance, it shelters rare alpine, Mediterranean and arctic flora. An extensive cave system runs beneath the surface, and Aillwee Cave is open to the public. (Open daily, May–early Nov. Phone 065 77036) [⚑] There are also the remains of graves, forts and crosses, the most famous of which is Poulnabrone Dolmen, dating from c. 2500 BC. The Burren Display Centre is beside Kilfenora's ruined 12thC cathedral and provides information on the area's geology and geography. (Open daily, Mar–Oct. Phone 065 88030) Lisdoonvarna was famous in Victorian times for its curative waters; you can still sample the 'eggy water' or take a sulphur bath. It is perhaps better known these days for its September Matchmaking Festival, when thousands gather in search of a partner.

❻ BUNRATTY

Bunratty Castle, one of the many castles built by the McNamaras in the 15thC, was a stronghold of the O'Brien clan for over two centuries. Its medieval banquets are a tourist favourite and it is the most famous of the Bunratty Folk Park buildings, which include an entire 19thC village street. (Open daily. Phone 061 361511) [⚑] Durty Nelly's is probably the area's best-known pub.

❼ ENNIS & ENVIRONS

The narrow streets of Clare's lively county town grew up around a 13thC Franciscan friary, built by the kings of Thomond on an island in the River Fergus, now Abbey St. Nearby restored Knappogue Castle is the 15thC flagship of 42 castles built by the McNamara clan. It opens at night for medieval banquets. (Open daily, May–Oct) The Craggaunowen Bronze Age Project at Craggaunowen Castle includes replicas of a crannog, ring fort and 5thC farmer's house.

❽ LOUGH DERG

The largest of the Shannon lakes. Killaloe's 12thC St. Flannan's Cathedral was restored in the 18thC, while the miniature chapel of St. Mo-Lua was removed from Friar's Island in 1929 when the island was submerged as part of a hydroelectric scheme. From Mountshannon boats leave for Holy Island (Inis Cealtra), where St. Caimin founded a 7thC monastery. Dromineer, on the lough's Co. Tipperary shores, is popular with water-sports enthusiasts. Charming Terryglass is built round a quay, with the ruins of a 14thC castle, and a 19thC church said to contain a relic of the True Cross.

❾ CLIFFS OF MOHER

These magnificent cliffs rise to 668 ft above the Atlantic, and stretch for 6 miles between Hag's Head and Doolin. O'Brien's Tower was built as a teahouse on the clifftop in 1835. A visitor centre in the car park is the only other 'official' source of the commercialism that has invaded this scenic spot.

❿ CASHEL

The 300 ft-high Rock of Cashel is one of Ireland's most spectacular sites. It was the seat of the kings of Munster from about the 4thC until 1101, when Muirceartaigh O'Brien handed it over to the Church, and Cashel became the province's ecclesiastical capital. The earliest building is the round tower, followed by Cormac's Chapel, which was consecrated in 1134. Other buildings include the 15thC Bishop's Palace. In Cashel town, ancient manuscripts and maps are displayed at the GPA Bolton Library. (Open Mon–Sat and Sun afternoon) The Folk Village is also worth a visit. (Open daily, May–Sep) [⚑] *i* 062 61333

⓫ CAHIR

Imposing Cahir Castle stands on the site of a 3rdC fort. It includes part of a stronghold built by Conor O'Brien in 1142. (Phone 052 41011) [⚑] Nearby is Swiss Cottage, a restored 19thC cottage in a beautiful wood. (Open Tue–Sun, mid June–Sep, Sat and Sun, Oct–early Nov)

⓬ MITCHELSTOWN CAVES

Discovered in 1833, the three caverns are up to 60 ft high. Spectacular formations include the 30 ft-high Tower of Babel. (Open daily. Phone 052 67246) [⚑]

⓭ GLEN OF AHERLOW

Tranquillity is the key word on this glorious winding drive from Galbally to Bansha through a glen between the Galtees and the Slievenamuck hills.

⓮ HOLY CROSS ABBEY

The abbey took its name from a relic of the True Cross, contained in a golden shrine here when the monastery was founded on the banks of the Suir in 1180. (Open daily)

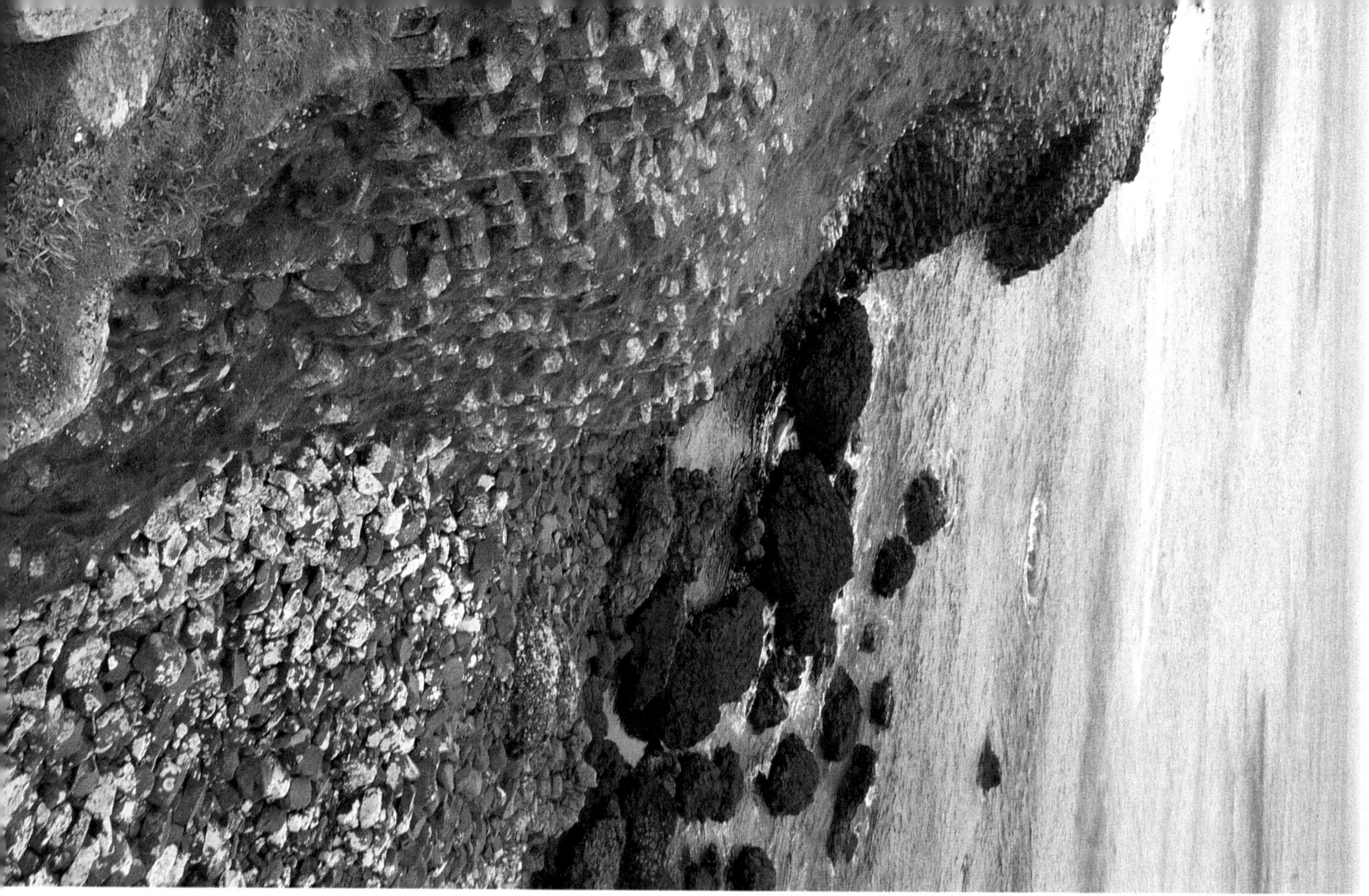

Myths and Legends

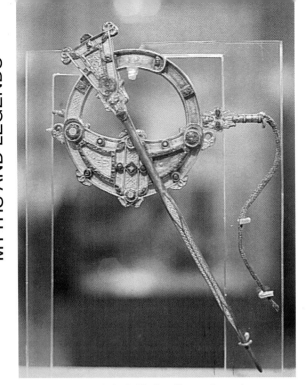

Tara Brooch and Ardagh Chalice (James Carney)

Myths, legends, folklore and customs have always played an important role in Irish life, from the days when the *fili*, bards and *seanchai* (storytellers) entertained people with poems, stories and songs about the mythical heroes, deeds, romances and follies of early Ireland, to modern times when tradition and customs, particularly religious, are still upheld.

Today only a few talented – and some untalented – *seanchai* still practice their skill, but their stories are usually 'tall tales', versions of which have delighted the Irish for thousands of years.

The earliest of the myths are based on the gods and goddesses of the ancient Celts, and include tales about the mystical Tuatha de Dannan and the battles they led against the Fomhoire, a race of sea pirates led by Balor of the Evil Eye, who was said to have had his base on Tory Island.

Another story recounts the tragic history of the children of the chieftain Lir who were turned into swans by their wicked stepmother and spent three hundred years on Lough Derravaragh, three hundred years on the Sea of Moyle between Ireland and Scotland and three hundred years on Inishglora off the Co. Mayo coast.

The Ulster Cycle of tales recounts the deeds of the Red Branch Knights and Cuchulainn. One of the first Irish sagas to be written down was the *Tain Bo Culainge* (*The Cattle Raid of Cooley*). The tale tells how Maeve, queen of Connaught, invaded Ulster to steal Cooley's great brown bull. The warriors of Ulster, however, were struck down by a magical illness and Cuchulainn alone defended the province until their recovery, fighting off the Connaught men even when mortally wounded.

Some of the greatest of the other heroic tales concern the Fianna, led by giant Finn MacCool, who were attributed with incredible feats of strength as

Preceding page and below: Giant's Causeway, Co. Antrim

Dunluce Castle, Co. Antrim

they fought off invaders, hunted wild animals and challenged each other to matches of skill and courage. Finn himself is said to have gained his wisdom when he burned his thumb cooking the salmon of knowledge for the seer Finneigas – who had spent seven years fishing for it – and put it in his mouth to cool. The Giant's Causeway, meanwhile, are stepping stones made by Finn to reach Scotland! One of the most popular of the tales, still taught in schools, is the love story of Grainne, given in marriage to the aged Finn, and Diarmuid, who she bewitches into eloping with her. The story of their pursuit across Ireland makes up 'An Toraiocht' (The Hunt) and many of the dolmens across the country are known as the beds of Diarmuid and Grainne.

The influence of Christianity quickly became evident in the tales of Ireland. In one story Oisin, son of Finn MacCool, enters Tir na nOg (Land of Eternal Youth) to be with the beautiful Niamh of the Golden Hair. After 300 years, which Oisin believes is only three, he yearns to see his homeland again, and he is given a white horse to make the journey, with the instructions that he must not dismount when he reaches Ireland. On his arrival he goes to the aid of a group of men attempting to move a great stone, but his saddle band snaps and he falls to the ground, turning into an old blind man. He then meets St. Patrick, to whom he recounts the great stories of his father, the Fianna and Tir na nOg. In the story of the children of Lir

it is the saint Mochaomhog who meets the swans on Inishglora, baptizing them as the bells of Christianity ring out and the spell of their enchantment is broken.

Hundreds of stories exist about St. Patrick and the other early saints, many of them about battles of wits with the pagan druids. Even today pilgrims visit holy shrines and wells throughout the country, seeking cures and other aid.

Irish Harp (James Carney)

Above: Derryclare Lough, Co. Galway

Below: King John's Castle, Limerick

King John's Castle, Carlingford, Co. Louth

Autograph Tree, Coole Park, Co. Galway

Glendalough, Co. Wicklow (James Carney)

Pagan rituals, however, still rear their heads, as in the ancient Puck Fair in Killorglin, Co. Kerry, an ancient fertility rite where a goat is crowned king.

The little people, *si* or fairies, are another topic which has fascinated centuries of Irish, and even many, otherwise worldly, modern farmers will not touch a rath (hummock) or tree because of their association with the 'little folk'.

The leprechauns were said to be both the guardians of the fairy treasure and the fairies' shoemakers, and also the bestowers of magical gifts on the occasional human. Many of the little people of folklore appear to have had a mischievous, if not downright evil, streak, often stealing human babies and leaving bad-tempered changelings behind, and injuring or bringing bad luck on anyone who intruded on their lives. The banshee – *bean si* or female spirit – is said to cry or keen to herald the death of a member of an Irish family, though usually only the descendants of the ancient Gaelic clans.

Healers are another feature of Irish life. Some are herbalists, others faith healers and a few even the seventh sons of seventh sons. A number of modern clergy have also been attributed with the gift of healing, and thousands of people will pack into local churches when they visit, many falling back in a faint when blessed by the healer. Healing is held in particular reverence by Ireland's travellers, a mainly nomadic people who have their own vibrant culture and customs and uphold many of the oldest religious traditions.

Wherever you travel, every other lake, castle, mountain and rock will have its story, or stories, be it about the little people, ancient battles or love stories, or even how a local outwitted the devil. This is a land where stories are often as important, if not more so, than actual history and contemporary authors, songwriters and poets still continue to explore the riches that have been handed down.

The Midlands are not always on the tourist's itinerary, often because their attractions are more subtle and they don't tie in with the foreign image of the so-called 'real Ireland'. But though the scenery, particularly for those who yearn for mountains and crashing seas, is not often a show-stopper, the region does contain some of Ireland's most pleasant and restful landscapes.

It is a region brimming with water, albeit the quieter waters of rivers, lakes, canals and soggy boglands. The great River Shannon marks the western boundaries of this territory, providing one of Ireland's finest amenities. But it also has a malicious streak, rising up regularly to flood fields and frustrate farmers.

Co. Longford is bordered to the south by one of the great lakes of the Shannon, Lough Ree, which also defines Co. Westmeath's western border, while loughs Sheelin, Lene, Derravaragh, Owel and Ennell cut through the county's heart.

As you would expect, the region is much favoured by anglers and water-sports enthusiasts, and one of the best, and most relaxing, ways to see it is by pleasure cruiser or narrowboat along the Grand Canal, heading east for the Barrow river or west for the Shannon.

The Slieve Bloom Mountains on the border between counties Laois and Offaly, though really hills – Arderin, the highest, is only 1734 ft – are one of the region's greatest attractions for walkers. Signposted trails include the 20 mile circular Slieve Bloom Way.

The bogs of the Midlands are another of their great assets. Some of Ireland's best preserved boglands are in Co. Offaly and in 1991 two enterprising Bord na Mona employees opened a tourist railway on Blackwater Bog, Shannonbridge – the Clonmacnoise and West Offaly Railway. Passengers are taken on a 6 mile, 45 minute guided trip starting from the Blackwater works. One side of the track is developed bog and the other is an untouched area of designated scientific interest. (Phone 0905 74114) In Co. Longford, archaeologists made a remarkable discovery when they uncovered an ancient roadway at Corlea Bog outside the village of Keenagh.

In ancient times Celtic Ireland is said to have been ruled from Tara in Co. Meath and the Hill of Uisneach, 10 miles from Mullingar towards Athlone, on which the Catstone, reputed to mark the centre of Ireland, stands. In Co. Offaly, however, that claim is also made for a spot near Birr.

Preceding page: Fore Abbey, Co. Westmeath

Locke's Distillery, Kilbeggan, Co. Westmeath

Lough Ennell, Co. Westmeath

The farming counties of Laois and Offaly, situated on Ireland's central limestone plain, carry the most marks of historical settlements: the Celtic church, the Vikings, the Anglo-Normans and most of all the 'planters'. The counties were chosen for the English Plantation experiments begun by Henry VIII but taken to new heights by his daughter Queen Mary. Land was confiscated from families, including the rebellious O'Moores of Laois and O'Connors of Offaly, and given to English settlers. Forts were built to enforce English control of the area and keep the Leinster Pale secure, the counties were renamed King's County and Queen's County, and bloody massacres and burnings continued for decades.

Longford

Ancient ecclesiastical connections are common, and Clonmacnoise in Co. Offaly is by far the most famous of the sites which remain. St. Patrick brought Christianity to Ardagh, Co. Longford in the 5thC, and left his nephew Mel behind as bishop. Ardagh remained the seat of the diocese until the 16thC, when it moved to Longford town. Behind today's imposing St. Mel's Cathedral in Longford is a small but fascinating diocesan museum, which houses penal crosses, and the 10thC St. Mel's Crozier, found in the original Ardagh cathedral. (Phone 043 46465) The remains of Durrow Abbey, north of Tullamore, mark the place where the *Book of Durrow*, an illuminated 7thC copy of the Gospels, was made.

It is also in the Midlands that you will find many of Ireland's neatest towns, including Tidy Town award-winners Ardagh and Newtowncashel in Co.

THE MIDLANDS

Longford, Clara in Co. Offaly, Tyrrellspass in Co. Westmeath, and Stradbally in Co. Laois, where the Irish Steam Preservation Society has a museum on the town green and a narrow-gauge railway runs through the grounds of Stradbally Hall.

The town of Abbeyleix in Co. Laois was remodelled in the 18thC around one main street, and its greatest attraction has to be Morrissey's pub, a unique and welcoming hostelry even by Irish standards. Banagher, Co. Offaly, where Charlotte Brontë honeymooned with husband Arthur Ben Nicholl, and Anthony Trollope served as post office surveyor, appears to have a pace as slow as the Shannon, here separating the town from Co. Galway.

At Timahoe is one of Ireland's best-preserved round towers, rising 96 ft through the trees, while in Ballybrittas a thatched cottage museum recalls more recent life styles in its two rooms. At Shannonbridge, in Co. Westmeath, a set of massive artillery fortifications date from the Napoleonic wars, while the peat-fired power station which looms over the town is an emblem of a more modern age.

Among the many gardens open to the public in the region are Heywood Gardens, Ballinakill, Co. Laois, which feature a sunken garden, terraces and pergola. (Phone 0502 33334)

The region also has associations with a number of literary figures, most notably Oliver Goldsmith. Edgeworthstown, formerly Mostrim, was renamed

Castlepollard, Co. Westmeath

after the Edgeworth family which included early 19thC author Maria Edgeworth, daughter of inventor and author Richard Lovell Edgeworth, who drew inspiration for her satirical novels, including the famous *Castle Rackrent,* from the local community.

Traditional music remains vibrant in many parts of the Midlands and the annual Harp Festival in Granard, Co. Longford – also the site of Ireland's highest Norman motte – attracts harpists, dancers and traditional Irish musicians from around the world every August.

Seven Wonders Bar, Fore

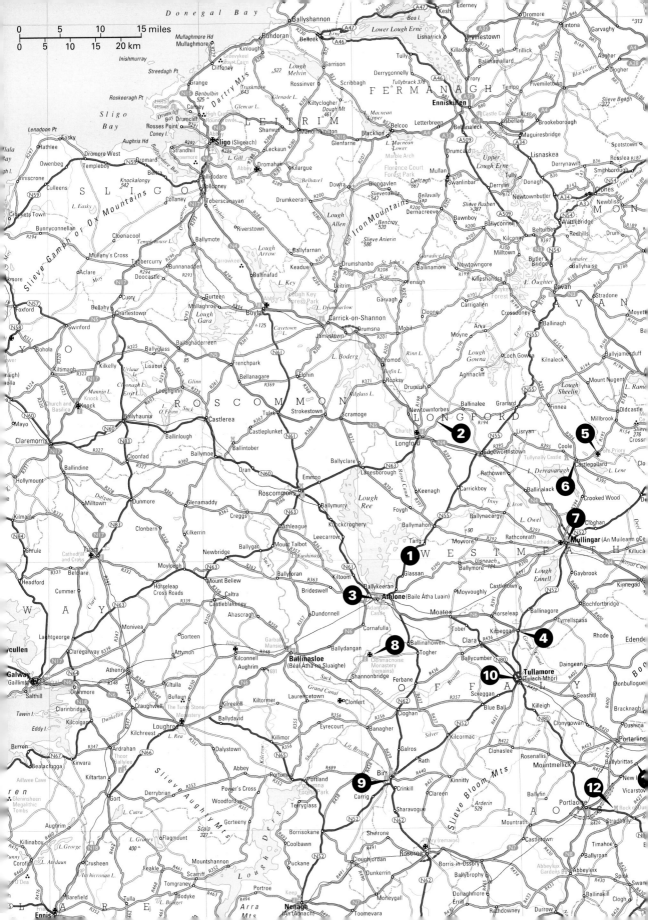

❶ GOLDSMITH COUNTRY

Born in the village of Pallas, off the Athlone–Ballymahon road, Oliver Goldsmith (1728–74) lived for most of his childhood near Auburn, Co. Westmeath. Although most of his working life was spent in London, it was from this area of neat villages, green pastures and lake shores that he received most of his inspiration. The stone of the 'busy mill' of his famous poem, *The Deserted Village*, can be seen at the entrance to the Three Jolly Pigeons pub on the Ballymahon road. Newtowncashel has a folk museum. (Phone 043 45698) Nearby Barley Harbour, on Lough Ree, is not only a beauty spot but also where to find Michael Casey, a sculptor who works with bog oak. Inchclearun, an island in Lough Ree, contains the remains of a monastic site founded by St. Diarmuid in the 6thC.

❷ CARRIGGLAS MANOR

Built in 1857 on the 650 acre estate of the Huguenot Lefroy family, this Gothic revival manor still contains its original furniture. Lively tours are given by the present-day Lefroys. (Open Thu–Mon afternoons, mid June–Sep. Phone 043 45156)

❸ ATHLONE

Now a major pleasure cruiser base, the River Shannon here divides the provinces of Leinster and Connacht. Due to its strategic importance, the town was the site of numerous battles. The castle which overlooked the main crossing point on the river for over 700 years (the main bridge is now upstream) is the town's oldest building. Built in 1210 by John de Gray, bishop of Norwich, it now houses a visitor and interpretative centre with exhibitions on the town's history, the wildlife of the Shannon and the town's most famous son, tenor John Count McCormack. (Open Mon–Sat, June–Sep. Phone 0902 72563) Glendeer Farm, near Drum, is a dairy farm with deer, pigs, goats, birds and old farm equipment. (Open Mon–Sat and Sun afternoon. Phone 0902 37147) [✕] *i* 0902 94630

❹ LOCKE'S DISTILLERY

Located on the Dublin–Galway road, this restored distillery is said to have been in existence since 1757, and recently has begun to distill whiskey again. There is a museum, art gallery and antique shop, and a cooper's workshop. (Open Mon–Sat and Sun afternoon. Phone 0506 32115/32154)

❺ FORE VALLEY

At Fore village, walk west into the valley to discover some of the Seven Wonders of Fore. First is the wood that will not burn – a dead branch – while nearby is the well of water that will not boil. Fore Priory was founded in AD 630 by St. Fechin and is the third wonder, being built on the 'quaking sod' (reclaimed bog). Other remains include St. Fechin's Church, where the massive 2 ton lintel stone is the fifth wonder, having been lifted there by a 'miracle'. A nearby hermit or anchorite's cell in a family vault is the seventh wonder. The remaining wonders are the mill without a race and the water that flows uphill from Lough Lene at the top of the valley.

❻ CASTLEPOLLARD

Laid out in English style around a green near the northern end of Lough Derravaragh, this town is popular with anglers. Tullynally Castle, just outside the village, has been home to the Pakenhams, earls of Longford, since 1655. It is the largest castle still occupied as a family home in Ireland. See the Victorian kitchen, 19thC gadgets, and one of the first British or Irish central-heating systems. (Garden: open daily. House: by appointment. Phone 044 61159)

❼ MULLINGAR

A market town, with the dominant twin spires of the Cathedral of Christ the King, favoured by anglers due to its proximity to loughs Ennell, Owel and Derravaragh. The Market Hall Museum has information about eccentric Adolphus Cooke, who thought he would be reincarnated as a bee! The Military Museum is also worth a look. Along the Tullamore road is Belvedere House and Gardens. The gardens include an ice house and the Jealous Wall, an artificial abbey ruin built by the 1st earl of Belvedere to block the view of nearby Rochfort House, his brother's home. (Grounds: open afternoons, May–Oct. Phone 044 40861/42820) *i* 044 4865

❽ CLONMACNOISE

Magnificently situated on the banks of the Shannon, this is one of Ireland's most important monastic and historical sites. It was founded in AD 548 and was once a great city and medieval university, surviving numerous raids until 1552, when it was destroyed by the English. The remains include a cathedral, seven church buildings and two round towers. There are also three high crosses and two holy wells. (Open daily, mid Mar–Oct) *i* 0905 74134

❾ BIRR

Birr is said to be almost at Ireland's geographic centre. The Seffin Stone, which once marked this disputed point, is now exhibited in John's Mall in the town, which owes its Georgian layout to the Parsons family, who built it around their 19thC castle. The castle, still home to the Parsons, earls of Rosse, is not open to the public but its ornamental gardens, with 34 ft box hedges and the remains of what was once the world's largest telescope, are. (Open daily. Phone 0509 20056) *i* 0509 20206

❿ TULLAMORE

A vibrant market town which is home to Irish Mist liqueur. Charleville Castle, built in 1798, is considered to be one of Ireland's finest Gothic-style houses. The main rooms include spectacular ceilings. (Open by appointment. Phone 0506 21279)

⓫ EMO COURT & GARDENS

A superb house, designed by James Gandon in 1760, set in extensive gardens containing many unusual trees and shrubs. (Gardens: open afternoons, Mar–Oct. House: open Mon afternoon. Phone 0502 26110)

⓬ ROCK OF DUNAMASE

The remains of a Celtic fortification crown this 150 ft rock overlooking the Valley of the O'Moores. The site appears on a Greek map of AD 140. The scene of many battles, it became a Norman stronghold in the 13thC, was reconstructed by the O'Moores in the 15thC, and was destroyed by Cromwellian troops in the 17thC. It is off the Portlaoise–Stradbally road.

The West

Preceding page: Kylemore Abbey, Co. Galway

Inishmore, Aran Islands

It is Connacht's rougher side, the wild, beautiful and often desolate Far West, that tourists are most familiar with. The inaccessibility of this inhospitable terrain proved almost impossible for invaders to overcome, and these coasts and mountains were one of the last regions of Ireland to surrender to the influence of the Tudor English. Gaeltachts – Irish-speaking areas – still survive today.

The Vikings never had much interest in the desolation of Connacht, preferring the richer pickings of Leinster and even Munster, while it took the Normans over a hundred years to gain any kind of hold on the region, and even then they avoided the extreme west.

'From the fury of the O'Flahertys, good Lord deliver us', read the sign over the entrance to Galway city during the 15th and 16thC, as the merchant tribes held themselves aloof from the 'mere Irish' outside the walls with a series of restrictive laws, trading with Continental Europe and defending themselves against hostile local clans. It was only after its sacking by Cromwellian troops and a later Williamite siege that Galway opened its streets to the rest of the west, and today it is its undisputed capital.

It was Cromwell too, who drove landowners across the Shannon after he had confiscated their lands, telling them to go 'to hell or to Connacht', and handing over huge tracts of land to his soldiers and other supporters.

The region was constantly the scene of unrest and rebellion. In 1798, over 1000 French troops landed at Killala, north of Ballina, led by General Humbert. They came to help the Irish overthrow English rule but, despite initial successes at Castlebar, local support was not sufficiently organized and the French eventually surrendered.

The impoverished west was also one of the areas where the Great Famine of the 19thC caused the most devastation, claiming millions of lives between 1846 and 1850, while over another million emigrated, many taking the dreadful 'coffin ships' to America.

Like many of the Europeans who are attracted to live in this region, the early and medieval Christian monks were enticed by its remoteness. They came in search of peace and quiet and found it at locations like Cong on the south Mayo border, the region's island-scattered lakes, and Inishglora, an island off the Mullet peninsula in Co. Mayo, which is still the site of the tiny church of St. Brendan the Navigator.

Lay people also chose to eke an existence on the islands of the west coast, of which the most famous are the Aran Islands. Inishbofin, once the home of Spanish pirate Don Bosco, and also used by Irish pirate Grace O'Malley, is a tranquil mixture of beaches, bogs and farmland. A ferry service operates from Cleggan near Clifden.

Most visitors to the west enter Co. Mayo from Clifden, along the breathtaking Sky Road, past beautiful Kylemore Abbey, with its grounds, restaurant and pottery, and round the edge of

Below: Westport, Co. Mayo

Killary Harbour into Leenane. Mayo is Ireland's third-largest county and much of its spectacular scenery is concentrated along the western coastline. Desolate Erris, the Mullet peninsula and land round Blacksod Bay and Broad Haven are a combination of apparently endless bogland, black hills, sparse pastureland, small farms and magnificent beaches.

The lowlands of the west, which venture from Roscommon into parts of Galway and Mayo, have for centuries been centres for cattle-rearing and agriculture, and the region's bustling market towns, such as Tuam and Loughrea, neat villages, and farms set among hedgerows and tree-lined lanes, are reminiscent of the Midlands on the far side of the Shannon. Portumna, which marks Connacht's last claim to the Shannon, was always a strategic crossing point on the great river but was only bridged in 1796.

The most sedate of the western counties is Roscommon, though there is something particularly pleasing about its lakes and Shannon scenery. North of the county, meanwhile, is one of the most splendid scenic drives in the country; the Arigna scenic drive cuts across the Kilronan Mountain on narrow winding roads round an area which until recently was the site of working coalfields.

Killary Harbour, Co. Mayo

Strokestown Park House, Co. Roscommon

Ballynahinch Lake, Co. Galway

Above and below: Knock, Co. Mayo

Horses play a number of important roles in the region. The Galway Races, held at Ballybrit in July, are the most famous in Ireland, and a lot more than mere horse races. Ballinasloe, Co. Galway, is host to a traditional horse fair every October, while the Connemara pony is celebrated at an annual show in Clifden every August.

Galway is also synonymous with the oyster. It was in Clarinbridge that the late Paddy Burke founded the international Oyster Festival, and his oyster tavern continues to draw the crowds. Nearby Morans of the Weir, a genuinely ancient

Galway

St. Nicholas' Collegiate Church, Galway

pub at the bottom of a byroad, is idyllic on a sunny day, and still bypassed by some, though not all, of the bus tours.

Nearby Coole Park, where Lady Gregory lived, at Gort is the Coole of W. B. Yeats' poems and just one of the region's literary claims to fame. Thoor Ballylee, where Yeats himself lived for a time, is close by and has been restored.

The statue of Gaelic writer Padraic O'Conaire sits in Eyre Sq. in Galway city, while near Moycullen is 17thC Ross Castle, where Violet Martin, the Martin Ross of the Somerville and Ross literary partnership (*The Irish RM*) was born. The Aran Islands, where short-story master Liam O'Flaherty was born, were also the source of inspiration for many of J. M. Synge's works. Oliver St. John Gogarty purchased Renvyle House near Letterfrack, Connemara, while the remains of Moore Hall on the shores of Co. Mayo's Lough Arrow were once the home of novelist George Moore. In Co. Roscommon the literary tradition began much earlier when the monks of Lough Key's Trinity Island compiled the *Annals of Lough Key*. Ireland's first president, Douglas Hyde, who translated ancient Gaelic poetry, was born and buried in Roscommon, and more recently the county provided the backdrop for a number of John McGahern's novels.

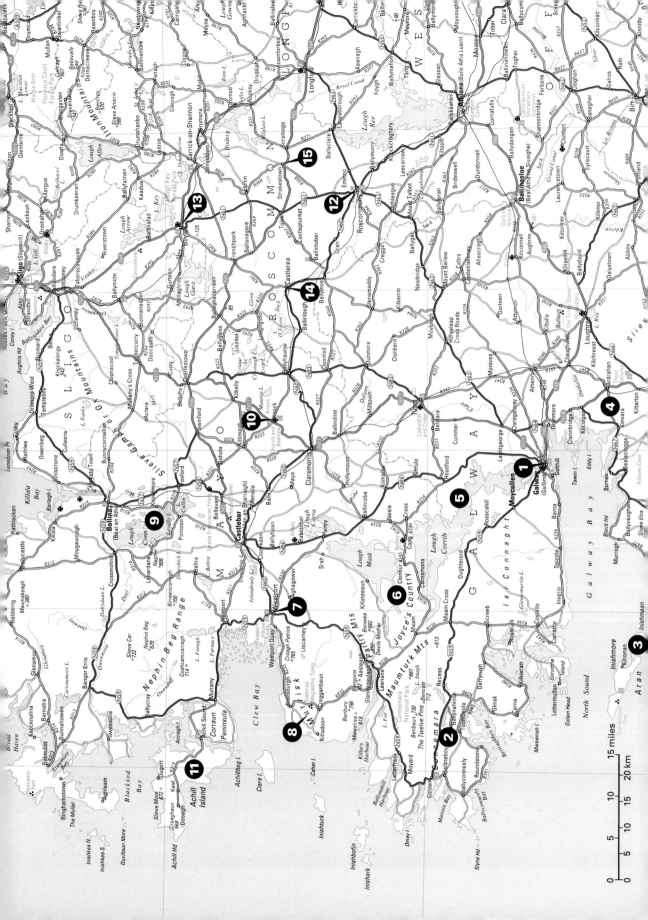

❶ GALWAY CITY

All that remains of the former city walls is Spanish Arch, built in 1594. Galway City Museum contains many old artefacts. (Open daily, summer. Phone 091 68151) Lynch's Castle, now a bank, is the former home of the premier of the 14 tribes of Galway. It was at St. Nicholas' Collegiate Church that Columbus heard Mass before setting off across the Atlantic. (Open Mon–Sat and Sun afternoon. Phone 091 64684) In Bowling Green is the home of Nora Barnacle, James Joyce's wife, which is now a museum. (Open Mon–Sat, May–Sep. Phone 091 64743) University College Galway, founded in 1845, still retains its original Tudor-style quad. (Phone 091 24414) The city is increasingly renowned for its growing arts tradition. *i* 091 63081

❷ CONNEMARA

One of Ireland's most hostile but beautiful regions. There are two main routes from Galway to Clifden. The Connemara Coastal Road leads from Barna and Carna to the desolate but spectacular landscape around the bays of Kilkieran, Bertraghboy and Ballyconneely. The North Connemara Route runs via Moycullen and Oughterard under the shadow of the majestic Twelve Pins. The 5000 acre Connemara National Park near Letterfrack includes four of the Pins. (Visitor centre: open daily, April–Oct. Phone 095 41054)

❸ ARAN ISLANDS

Dun Aengus, a fort on Inishmore, is the islands' most important antiquity. Inishmaan is the most colourful of the islands and Inisheer is dominated by a huge rock formation, crowned by the ruins of a 15thC castle. Fishing is done from *currachs*, fragile-looking boats covered in tarred canvas. Aer Arann operates regular air services to Inishmore. (Phone 091 55437) Daily ferries operate from Galway, Spiddle, Rossaveal and Doolin.

❹ SOUTHERN GALWAY

Coole Park near Gort was the former home of Lady Augusta Gregory, a member of the 20thC Anglo-Irish literary and dramatic revival, and a favourite retreat for writers including W. B. Yeats. (Open daily) Five miles from Gort is Thoor Ballylee, a 16thC tower house bought by Yeats in 1917. (Open daily, May–Sep) Round the bay is 16thC Dunguaire Castle. (Open daily, mid April–Sep) The annual Gathering of the Boats is held in Kinvara, featuring the county's traditional craft, the Galway hooker.

❺ LOUGH CORRIB

One of the chain of lakes that divides Connacht's fertile eastern lowlands from the rugged west. Salmon, trout and pike are plentiful. Aughnanure Castle near Oughterard was built in the 15thC by the O'Flahertys. (Open daily, mid June–mid Sep) Inchagoill is probably the most beautiful of the lough's islands. Boats operate from near Cong and Oughterard.

❻ JOYCE'S COUNTRY

A Welsh family who settled here in the 13thC gave this border area its name, the scene of many battles between the clans of the northeastern lowlands and the western mountains. Picturesque Cong, location for the film *The Quiet Man*, is to the east.

❼ WESTPORT

This elegant town was designed by the Georgian architect William Wyatt, and The Mall is one of Ireland's most attractive streets. Westport House is one of the few 'Big Houses' left in the region. There is also a zoo. (Open afternoons, May–Sep) [🏊]

❽ BARONY OF MURRISK

The barony is north of Killary Harbour, a 10 mile-long fjord, and the tiny village of Leenane. The lovely Aasleagh Falls are on the road to Louisburgh, where the interpretative centre is dedicated to 16thC pirate queen Grace O'Malley. (Open daily, June–mid Oct) Boats leave from Roonagh Quay for Clare Island, O'Malley's former home. In Murrisk a footpath leads up 2510 ft Croagh Patrick. A pilgrimage takes place to the summit on the last Sunday in July.

❾ LOUGH CONN

This lake is famous for its salmon and brown trout. In Foxford are the Providence Woollen Mills where rugs have been made since 1892.

❿ KNOCK

In 1879 several people claimed to see a vision of the Blessed Virgin Mary, St. Joseph, St. John the Evangelist and the Lamb of God near the local church, and thousands of pilgrims now flock here. A folk museum depicts rural life in the area. (Open daily, May–Oct)

⓫ ACHILL ISLAND

Ireland's largest island, joined to the mainland by bridge since 1988, is dominated by Slieve More and Croaghaun. Its lively resorts, golden beaches, towering cliffs and moorland are unsurpassed – in good weather.

⓬ ROSCOMMON

The ruins of a Dominican priory can be seen in the grounds of the Abbey Hotel. Roscommon Castle was built in 1269, burnt in 1273, and rebuilt in 1280. The Bank of Ireland which divides Main St served formerly as the courthouse, and then the Catholic church until 1903. James Harlow's shop and bar on Main St is a treasure trove of household paraphernalia.

⓭ BOYLE

Boyle is a popular angling base due to its site between loughs Key and Gara. Boyle Abbey is one of the finest Cistercian remains in Ireland. (Open daily, mid June–mid Sep) Just outside the town is the 300 hectare Lough Key Forest Park. (Open daily. Phone 079 62212/62214) [🏊]

⓮ CASTLEREA

In wooded land on the banks of the Suck. Clonalis House is the ancestral home of the O'Conor clan, reputed to be Europe's oldest family. Its 45 rooms contain a priceless archive. (Open Mon–Sat and Sun afternoon, June–Sep. Phone 0907 20014)

⓯ STROKESTOWN

The main street of this planned village leads to the gates of fascinating Strokestown Park House, built in 1800. (Open Tue–Sun afternoons, June–mid Sep. Phone 078 33013) The County Heritage and Genealogical Centre has a display on the site of Rathcroghan, an ancient coronation and burial site of Irish kings.

Preceding page and above: Glenveagh Castle, Co. Donegal

Few visitors come away untouched by the magic of Ireland's northwest corner, sure in the knowledge that they have stumbled across somewhere very special.

The region has many beauty spots, among them the Glenaniff Falls near Rossinver in Co. Leitrim; the Assaroe Falls near Ballyshannon; and the drive from Crolly to Glenveagh along Lough Nacung in the shadow of Errigal Mountain. But it is also a region where you are likely to discover your own idyll unmentioned in any guide, be it a deserted beach or cove, lake view or mountain valley.

The counties of the northwest are divided by their provincial allegiances. Donegal is one of the three Ulster counties that stayed in the Republic, while Sligo and Leitrim belong to Connacht. For years, until partition, Donegal looked to Derry as its city, while the people of Londonderry even today regard the Inishowen peninsula as their personal playground.

Co. Leitrim also borders Northern Ireland, though virtually all connecting roads have been closed. Many border towns, meanwhile, have a dual identity, with Pettigoe in Co. Donegal being literally carved up between the North and the Republic.

Historical differences aside, the geographical contrasts are also prominent, with the quieter attractions of the two more southern counties at variance with the wild beauty of Co. Donegal.

One of the region's best-known landmarks is Benbulben, the 1722 ft 'table-top' mountain which dominates the landscape around Sligo town. W. B. Yeats was one of this mountain's greatest fans and his wish to be buried in its sight was granted when he was interred at Drumcliff.

Co. Sligo contains some of the greatest concentrations of prehistoric sites in Ireland, at locations like Carrowkeel, Carrowmore and Creevykeel, and the remains of over two hundred 2000-year-

Lough Swilly, Co. Donegal

old crannogs have been found in Lough Gara. Inishmurray, inhabited until 1947, also contains many antiquities, including one of the country's oldest churches.

Leitrim is often called the 'forgotten county', for this tiny area is hugely underpopulated due to massive emigration, forced by the absence of industry and small farm holdings unable to support large families. But it is fighting back against all the odds.

The county is cut by Lough Allen which separates the mountains and valleys of the north from

Malin Beg, Co. Donegal

the Iron Mountains, bogs and hilly land of the south. Among its villages, frequented largely by anglers, are Leitrim itself, Ballinagleragh, Ballinamore, Drumkeeran, Kinlough and pretty Drumshanbo. Tullaghan, meanwhile, offers fishing in both the Atlantic and in the rivers Duff and Drowes.

One of Leitrim's greatest assets is the town of Carrick-on-Shannon, a lively angling and boating centre much loved by traditional musicians. Ireland's smallest church, the Costello Chapel, built in memory of Josephine Costello by her husband, is at the corner where Bridge St and Main St meet.

In ancient times it was in the pretty village of Dromahair on the River Bonet that the O'Rourke kings of Breifne had their seat. It was from here in 1152 that Dervogilla O'Rourke eloped with Dermot McMurrough, king of Leinster. She later returned to her husband but when McMurrough was banished by the high king he sought the aid of King Henry II, a move that prompted the Norman invasion of Ireland.

The beauties of Co. Donegal are almost all on a grand scale, and it sometimes seems like a vast, desolate mass of bogs, gushing streams, rocky peaks, mountain passes, sombre lakes and massive cliffs and headlands, among them Slieve League, Fanad Head and Bloody Foreland – named after the colour its stone turns in the setting sun.

Donegal town on the River Eske was the seat of the O'Donnells from the Middle Ages to the 17thC, and after they fled to Europe in 1607 it was 'planted' by Sir Basil Brooke. The ruins of the town castle, which include the tower built by Red Hugh O'Donnell in 1505, are beside the old three-sided marketplace, The Diamond.

Lough Gill, Co. Sligo

Letterkenny, Co. Donegal

The village of Creeslough overlooks the inlet of Sheep Haven and is an ideal base for climbing Slieve Muckish. The picturesque Duntally Bridge and waterfall are just outside the village and Doe Castle, a 15thC McSweeney fortress, commands the nearby peninsula.

Lough Swilly divides the Inishowen and Fanad peninsulas. Ramelton, sited where the Leannan river flows into the lough, is where Francie Mackemie, founder of the Presbyterian Church in North America, was born. The meeting house where he worshipped before moving to Virginia in 1683 now houses a museum. It was from the seaside resort of Rathmullan on the lough that the earls of Tyrone (O'Neills) and Tyrconnell (O'Donnells) sailed to Europe in 1607 during the Flight of the Earls, after the confiscation of their lands.

The region's beaches are some of the finest in the world, and include Rosses Point, Rossnowlagh and the strands of the magical Rosguill peninsula. Tullan Strand, bounded at one end by wonderful rock formations, at Bundoran is one of the most popular, drawing thousands of holiday-makers every year.

Lough Foyle

Letterkenny, dominated by the 215 ft spire of its Catholic cathedral, is the county's commercial and administrative centre, and contains one of the country's longest main streets. Raphoe also has a 'diamond' marketplace at its centre, while its 18thC cathedral still contains the only consistory court where marriage licences were issued and legal arguments over wills settled until the 19thC. Near the town on Tops Hill are the 64 standing stones of the Beltany Stone Circle, dating from c. 1800 BC.

Killybegs is the largest, and most pungent, of the region's fishing ports, and the scenic route from Killybegs to Carrick is probably one of the most spectacular coastal drives in Ireland. Pretty Ardara is a centre for hand-woven tweeds and knitwear, while Glenties is just one of the region's many handsome Plantation villages.

Dungloe is the capital of the Rosses, a rocky, lake-sprinkled Gaeltacht region which stretches out to the coast at Burtonport and up to Crolly, home of the musical Brennan or O'Braonain family, best known to the world as the group Clannad.

The Gaeltacht island of Arranmore is only a mile from Burtonport, while Gweedore to the north, another Gaeltacht area, takes in the tiny old port of Bunbeg, Derrybeg village and Bloody Foreland.

A Game of Hurley

Bunglas, Co. Donegal

Above: Donegal   *Below:* Kilcar, Co. Donegal

Dromod, Co. Leitrim

THE NORTHWEST

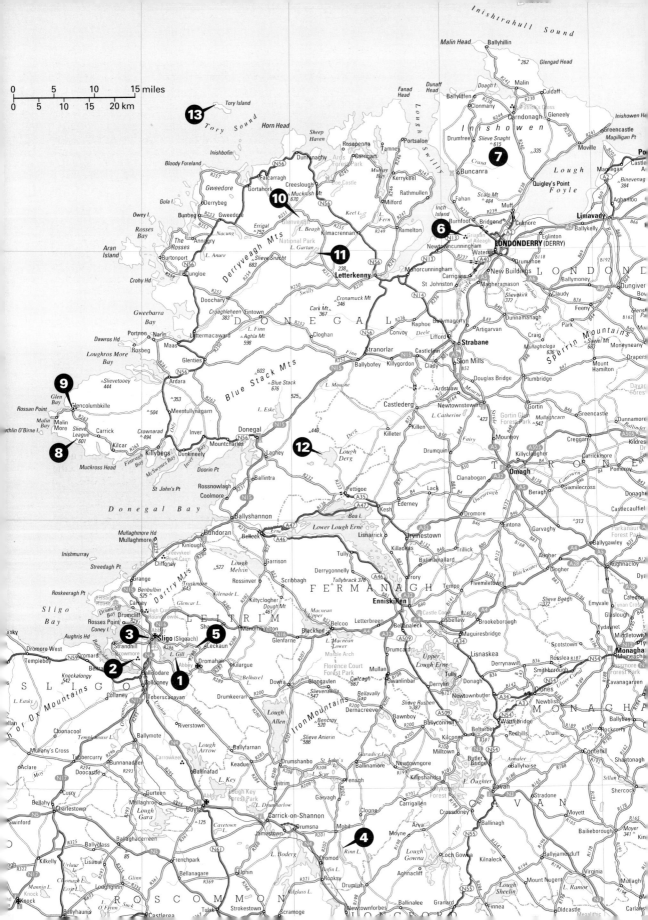

❶ LOUGH GILL

The drive round this lovely lake is a 'must' for Yeats fans. Among its attractions are the Rock of Dooney (*The Fiddler of Dooney*), Slish Wood (*The Stolen Child*) and Inishfree (*The Lake Isle of Inishfree*). At Tobernalt Holy Well and Shrine, the marks on the Mass rock were, according to the legend, made by St. Patrick's fingers.

❷ CARROWMORE MEGALITHIC TOMBS

This area southwest of Sligo town is considered to have the greatest concentration of megalithic tombs and monuments in Europe. It is believed that over 85 tombs survived until the 19thC, when they were rifled by amateur archaeologists. Today, 60 tombs have been located. There is a visitor centre with an audiovisual display and guided tours. (Open daily, June–Sep. Phone 071 64186)

❸ SLIGO TOWN

Sited on the Garavogue river, the settlement was given in 1235 to Maurice Fitzgerald, who built a castle and founded a Dominican friary. Ireland's largest collection of Jack B. Yeats paintings is in the Sligo Museum and Gallery, and a Yeats Museum is open during the summer. The Yeats Building on Douglas Hyde Bridge is the venue for an annual Yeats Summer School. *i* 071 61201

❹ LOUGH RINN HOUSE & GARDENS

The restored home of the infamous lords of Leitrim is near Mohil. The estate includes Victorian gardens, a 16thC castle ruin, a dolmen and 600 acres of lakes. (Open daily, April–Aug. Phone 078 31427) [☎]

❺ PARKE'S CASTLE

On Lough Gill's northeast shores, this is considered to be Ireland's finest Plantation castle. It houses an interpretative centre for Leitrim and Sligo's national monuments. (Open daily, June–Sep. Phone 071 64186)

❻ GRIANAN OF AILEAGH

This fort is set on top of 800 ft Greenan Hill and has panoramic views over loughs Foyle and Swilly. The entire enclosure covers 4 acres. Its name means 'sun palace', and the kingdom of Aileagh included Co. Donegal and most of Londonderry, Tyrone and Armagh, over which the kings of Ulster ruled. Built c. 1700 BC, possibly as a druids' sun temple, it was occupied until the 12thC. The site was wrecked in 1101 and restored in the 19thC. (Open daily)

❼ INISHOWEN PENINSULA

This peninsula separates loughs Foyle and Swilly, and contains some of the country's most unspoilt scenery. The border extends up past Culmore Point on the east. Buncrana is besieged in summer, its attraction being its beach which stretches down to lovely Fahan and north to Stragill. The town has a Vintage Car and Carriage Museum. (Open daily, June–Sep. Phone 077 61130) [☎] Moville was a former port of call for transatlantic liners. In the churchyard on the outskirts of Carndonagh is the ornate 7thC Donagh Cross, also known as St. Patrick's Cross, and a number of other decorated stones. Fort Dunree, built in the early 1800s, crowns Dunree Head and now contains a military museum. (Open daily, June–Sep. Phone 074 24613) At Malin Head, Ireland's most northerly point, the cliffs rise to 200 ft. The head's highest point, over 360 ft, is called Banba's Crown after an ancient pagan queen. Ali Farren's, a fishermen's pub, is the country's most northerly bar. Malin's ten-arch bridge, built in the mid-18thC, is the second-longest stone bridge in Ireland.

❽ SLIEVE LEAGUE

Rising 2000 ft above the Atlantic, these incredible cliffs afford views over 5 counties. Only the fit, and those with a head for heights, should attempt the often dangerous cliff walk. Ask at Teelin or Carrick for directions or to hire a guide. There is a spectacular drive from Carrick to the eastern end of Slieve League.

❾ GLENCOLUMBKILLE

This valley was the 6thC retreat of St. Columbcille, or Columba, and locals still make annual pilgrimages barefoot round the area's cross-inscribed slabs, beginning at 2400 on 9 June. More recently it became the site of the rural cooperative founded by Fr James MacDyer to try to slow emigration. The folk park he began includes an archaeological walk taking in a Mass rock, limekiln and tower. There are also replicas of an old National School, a shebeen where you can sample seaweed wine and a sweathouse, a medieval Irish sauna. (Open daily, Easter–Sep. Phone 073 30017) [☎]

❿ GLENVEAGH NATIONAL PARK

This 10,000 hectare park, centred on a 19thC castle overlooking Lough Veagh, has an interpretative centre, ornate gardens and vast expanses of mountains, glens and lakes to explore. A 'must'. (Open daily, April–Oct. Phone 074 37088) [☎]

⓫ LOUGH GARTAN

St. Columb's on Lough Gartan contains a remarkable collection of artworks, furniture, pottery and glass, while its grounds feature rare plants. Adjacent is the Glebe Gallery, with works by Hill, Yeats and many others. (Open daily, May–Sep. Phone 074 37071) The nearby Columbcille Centre traces the saint's life. The saint himself was born nearby. He is said to have slept on the large flagstone which marks the spot and given it the power to cure loneliness.

⓬ LOUGH DERG

In a cave on Station Island in this remote lake near Pettigoe, St. Patrick is said to have fasted for 40 days and nights and had a vision of hell and purgatory, before his penance drove the devil from his last stronghold in Ireland. Modern pilgrims travel to the island every summer to fast, pray without sleep and perform the stations, a barefoot circuit. Only pilgrims are allowed on the island.

⓭ TORY ISLAND

This island has been populated for at least 4000 years and St. Columbcille founded a monastery here in the 6thC, of which a round tower and cross remain. During the winter the 120 inhabitants are often cut off from the mainland. Ask about boats at Bunbeg or Magheraroarty.

Belfast

BELFAST

Ireland's second capital is best known throughout the world as a city plagued by terrorism and sectarianism, one of the main centres of the ongoing 'Troubles'. But the often gruesome scenes flashed across television screens worldwide are by no means the full picture. For though Belfast life is not quite as rosy as that painted by the tourist board, it is a vibrant and exciting historical city, packed with beautiful buildings and parks, wonderful restaurants, year-round top theatrical and musical events, and great pubs.

Ireland's largest seaport began as a tiny settlement around a crossing on the River Farset, which once ran down what is now High St, site of Belfast's 'Big Ben', the Albert Clock Tower. The Norsemen were among the first to be attracted by the area's advantages as a trading post, followed by the invasion of the Anglo-Normans in 1171, when John de Courcy was established as earl of Ulster, and right throughout the Middle Ages bids for control of the area resulted in many bloody disputes. The town grew slowly around the mouth

Grand Opera House

St. Anne's Cathedral

Queen's University

of the Lagan, and even when a charter was granted by James I in 1631, Belfast was little more than a village. The arrival of the French Huguenots at the end of the 17thC, however, established a local linen industry. Although the town was almost totally gutted by fire in 1708, the textile business continued to grow, along with a booming shipbuilding trade, and rope-making, engineering and tobacco businesses. The town's size doubled every ten years; by the time it received city status from Queen Victoria in 1888 its population had exceeded 208,000, and by the turn of the century had surpassed Dublin's.

Preceding spread: City Hall

Above: Belfast City Centre

Below: City Hall

Above: Nick's Warehouse

Today, though in great decline, the shipbuilding industry is still vital to the city's economy, and it is Samson and Goliath, the two gigantic cranes of the Harland and Wolff shipyard, which dominate Belfast's skyline. It was at this great yard, established in 1859, that many of the great passenger liners, including the ill-fated *Titanic*, were built.

Sectarianism is a relatively new development in Belfast. During the 18thC it was here that the nationalist society, the United Irishmen, was founded by Presbyterian Ulstermen, while local Protestants contributed generously to a building fund for a new Catholic church. But as the 19thC progressed many Presbyterian ministers began open attacks on Catholicism, encouraged by the recent achievement of Catholic emancipation, an increase in the Catholic population, and the rise of the Orange Order. Belfast became the centre of Unionist opposition to Home Rule, and as the divisions grew greater so did the violence.

The most obvious divides today are in West Belfast. But the barricades and security zones are almost everywhere. Bags will be checked and you are likely to be frisked entering city centre shopping areas, and parking in the city is very restricted.

However, unlike many other European cities, the chances of being mugged or robbed are slim. Apart from paramilitary organized crimes and sectarian violence, the crime rate is low. And the ordinary citizens of this lovely city, anxious to get on with

their lives in peace, will provide as friendly a welcome as any you receive throughout the entire island.

The city itself is situated in tranquil hilly countryside, with Cave Hill to the north, Black Mountain to the west and the fertile Lagan Valley to the south. Dixon Park, with its thousands of rose bushes, and the Lagan Valley Park, with its 9 miles of towpath, are just two of the wonderful open areas to be enjoyed.

Above and below: Crown Liquor Saloon

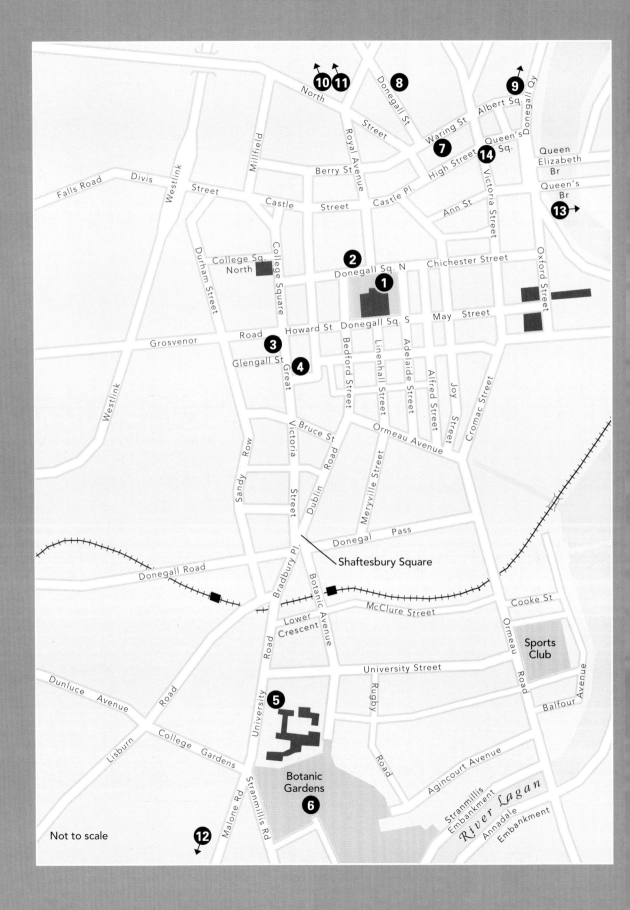

North

Donegall St

8

10 **11**

Albert Sq.

9

Donegall Qy

Millfield

Westlink

Royal Avenue

Berry St

Waring St

High Street

7

Queen's
Sq.

14

Queen
Elizabeth
Br

Falls Road

Divis

Westlink

Street

Castle

Street

Castle Pl.

Castle Pl.

Ann St

Victoria Street

Queen's
Br

13

Durham Street

College Sq.
North

College Square

Donegall Sq. N

2

Chichester Street

Oxford Street

Grosvenor

Road

Howard St

Donegall Sq. S

1

May Street

3

Glengall St

4

Great

Bedford Street

Linenhall Street

Adelaide Street

Alfred Street

Joy Street

Cromac Street

Sandy Row

Victoria Street

Bruce St

Dublin Road

Meryville Street

Ormeau Avenue

Donegal Pass

Shaftesbury Square

Donegall Road

Bradbury Pl.

Botanic Avenue

Lower
Crescent

McClure Street

Cooke St

Ormeau Road

Sports
Club

Dunluce Avenue

Lisburn Road

College Gardens

University Road

University Street

Rugby Road

Agincourt Avenue

Balfour Avenue

Malone Rd

Stranmillis Rd

5

Botanic
Gardens

6

Stranmillis
Embankment

Annadale
Embankment

River Lagan

12

Not to scale

❶ CITY HALL

Completed in 1906 after 8 years' work, it is built predominantly in Portland stone and its central copper dome rises to 173 ft. Inside, its main attractions include marble stairs and floors, a Rococo plasterwork ceiling, and stained-glass windows depicting the history of Belfast Corporation. A mural illustrates the city's traditional industries, and the council chambers and visitors' gallery have beautifully carved oak panelling. (Guided tours: book in advance. Phone 0232 320202, ext. 2227)

❷ LINEN HALL LIBRARY

Founded in 1788 by the Belfast Society for Promoting Knowledge, the city's oldest public library was originally sited in White Linen Hall on the site of the current City Hall. Its contents include a Robert Burns collection, over 20,000 important Irish volumes and extensive genealogical records. The current building was originally a linen warehouse. (Open Mon–Sat. Phone 0232 321707)

❸ GRAND OPERA HOUSE

Lavishly designed inside and out in 1894 by Robert Matcham, who opted for an Eastern motif. The building was restored during the 1970s, re-opening after almost 10 years in 1980. More recently it was forced to close temporarily due to bomb damage. It hosts a wide variety of shows, ranging from drama, pop concerts, ballet and opera to pantomime. (Phone 0232 241919)

❹ CROWN LIQUOR SALOON

Now in the care of the National Trust, this spectacular Victorian pub still has gaslights, ornate glasswork and tiles, brass pipes and taps, carved oak and snugs. It was originally designed as a railway tavern in 1855 by an architecture student from Banbridge who was influenced by his travels in Spain and Italy. (Open 1130–2300 Mon–Sat, 1230–1430, 1900–2200 Sun. Phone 0232 249476)

❺ QUEEN'S UNIVERSITY

Architect Charles Lanyon modelled the main college building, with Tudor cloisters and mullioned windows, on Magdalen College in Oxford. It is possible to visit the entrance hall and a gallery in the central tower. (Open daily. Phone 0232 245133)

❻ BOTANIC GARDENS

The best features of these gardens set in 38 acres are probably the rose garden and herbaceous borders. Coffee, banana and cotton plants grow in the Victorian Palm House, which is older than the great palm house at Kew Gardens and said to be the earliest surviving example of cast iron and curvilinear glass in the world. Opposite is the Tropical Ravine and 'jungle' environment. (Gardens: open daily. Palm House: daily Mon–Fri and Sat and Sun afternoons. Phone 0232 324902) Also in the gardens is the Ulster Museum. Highlights include the gold and silver jewellery recovered in 1967 from the Armada treasure ship, *Girona*, which was wrecked off the Giant's Causeway in 1588. Its collections of Irish and international art are also impressive. (Open daily Mon–Fri and Sat and Sun afternoons. Phone 0232 381251) [☂]

❼ WAR MEMORIAL BUILDING

The War Memorial Building houses both the Home Front Heritage Centre (phone 0232 310278), which features exhibits from World War II, including an incendiary bomb which was dropped on Belfast in 1941, and the Royal Ulster Rifles Museum (phone 0232 232086), which preserves memorabilia of this famous regiment, first raised in 1793, and which joined with other Irish regiments in 1968 to form the Royal Irish Rangers. (Open Mon–Fri)

❽ ST. ANNE'S CATHEDRAL

Begun in 1899 and completed in 1927, this Anglican cathedral, built on the site of the old parish church, features splendid mosaics, including one commemorating St. Patrick's landing at Saul in AD 432. The baptistry roof is made from 15,000 pieces of glass representing the Creation, and the floor of the Chapel of the Holy Spirit is laid with stones from each of the 32 counties of Ireland. (Open daily)

❾ SINCLAIR SEAMEN'S CHURCH

Designed by Charles Lanyon, architect of both the Customs House and Queen's University. Opened in 1853, it is a maritime masterpiece. The pulpit is a ship's prow, the organ has port and starboard lights, and model ships and a lighthouse circle the ceiling. (Open Wed afternoon, summer, and Sun during services. Phone 0232 757730)

❿ CAVE HILL

Stately Belfast Castle, completed in 1870 and set in formal gardens, is on the slopes of the hill. The castle (now a restaurant) was presented to the city by the 9th Lord Shaftesbury. There are panoramic views of the city and beyond from the summit, where the flat-topped stronghold, McArt's Fort, is guarded by cliffs on two sides. There are also five ancient caves. Access from Belfast Castle car park.

⓫ BELFAST ZOO

A mountain park beautifully sited on Cave Hill overlooking the city, with chimps, bears and birds, and an aquatic complex with penguins, sea lions and polar bears. (Open daily. Phone 0232 776277) [☂]

⓬ GIANT'S RING

This huge prehistoric earthwork, over 550 ft in diameter, is near Shaw's Bridge car park, and has a dolmen at its centre. It was also used as a horse-racing venue during the 18thC.

⓭ BELFAST TRANSPORT MUSEUM

The museum commemorates over 200 years of Irish transport. Its most prized exhibit is *Old Maeve*, the largest locomotive ever built in Ireland. There are also vintage cars, trams and motorcycles. (Open Mon–Sat. Phone 0232 451519) [☂]

⓮ ALBERT MEMORIAL CLOCK TOWER

Belfast's 'Big Ben' at the end of High St was designed by William Barne in 1869 and depicts Prince Albert in flowing robes guarded by four lions. The foundations of the clock tower are gradually sinking.

County Museum, Armagh

Above and below: Ulster-American Folk Park

Preceding page: Bishop's Gate, Downhill, Co. Derry

Under the Anglo-Irish Treaty of 1921, Ulster was divided. The six counties of Antrim, Armagh, Down, Londonderry, Tyrone and Fermanagh became Northern Ireland, while Donegal, Cavan and Monaghan joined Ireland's 23 other counties in the Free State, which later became the Republic of Ireland.

Northern Ireland contains some of the most beautiful and bewitching scenery in the entire island. If time is limited, the coastal drive from north of Londonderry to Belfast and the Fermanagh lakeland should be high priorities, but the attractions are endless and there is little evidence outside border areas of the bloody conflict which has made this region infamous.

In ancient times Ulster was ruled from Eamhain Macha or Navan Fort, near Armagh city, by a series of Celtic monarchs, and many of Ireland's legends are based around the exploits of these kings and queens and their warriors, the Red Branch Knights.

It was also to Ulster that Christianity first came. St. Patrick is believed to have returned to Ireland as a missionary in AD 432, landing at Strangford Lough near Saul, where he built his first church. And it was probably the enticement of the riches contained in some of the monasteries which sprung up throughout Ulster that brought the Vikings almost 400 years later, when they carried out their first raid on Rathlin Island.

The Anglo-Normans were the next arrivals in Ulster, and the castle built by John de Courcy in 1180 at Carrickfergus served as the seat of English power in the north for over 400 years, remaining in use until 1928. But the great Irish clans, which included the powerful O'Neills and McDonnells, were not brought under complete control until the Tudor Plantations which began in 1603. The lands of families which were not loyal to the Crown were taken and 'planted' with Scottish and English settlers, the ascendants of many of today's Loyalists.

Today, one of the most obvious signs of the region's divisions is the annual marches, unique to the North. On 12 July every year, Ulster's Orangemen don their bowler hats and take to the streets behind the pipe bands and Lambeg drums.

Above: Ballintoy Harbour   *Below:* Carrickarede

Castlerock, Co. Derry

Lough Erne, Co. Fermanagh

The Ancient Order of the Hibernians are the Catholic equivalent of the Orange Order. They march on Lady's Day, the Church Feast of the Assumption, on 15 August. In Londonderry the city's Apprentice Boys march on 12 August to commemorate the occasion in 1688 when 13 apprentices slammed the city gates on the soldiers of James I, sent to take over the city. In April the following year the city was put under siege by James himself for 105 days.

Chief among the region's beauty spots are the Mourne Mountains in the southeast, the Glens of Antrim in the northeast, and the area in Fermanagh

105

Crom Old Castle, Co. Fermanagh

where the River Erne bursts into lower and upper Lough Erne. The Sperrin Mountains border the peaceful moors and forests of Co. Tyrone, and on the northern coast is the Giant's Causeway, Ireland's only World Heritage Site.

Lough Neagh, famous for its eels, covers 153 square miles and is the largest lake in Britain and Ireland. Five of the North's counties touch upon its shores. According to legend, it was formed when

Mussenden Temple, Downhill, Co. Derry

the giant Finn MacCool scooped out a huge lump of earth and threw it into the Irish sea. The lump became the Isle of Man!

Among the gentle hills between Banbridge and Rathfriarland in Co. Down is the Brontë homeland, where Patrick, father of the famous novelists, and numerous other relations were born.

Magilligan Strand, overlooked by Magilligan Point, near Londonderry, is Ireland's longest beach, and among the region's many forest parks and gardens are Slieve Gullion Forest Park southwest of Newry, and the splendid Rowallane Gardens at Saintfield, near Ballynahinch.

Apart from its two cities, Northern Ireland has many elegant towns, such as Georgian Hillsborough, south of Belfast, which centres on Hillsborough Castle, the former governor's residence, used now only for State occasions. Pretty villages are also ten a penny. One of the region's most scenic beauty spots is Glenoe village near Larne and its spectacular waterfall.

One of the great joys of visiting Northern Ireland, however, is the solitude and tranquillity it offers. Away from the largest tourist attractions you will rarely be confronted by bus-loads of tourists. Relatively few people, even from the adjacent Republic, have discovered the charm of Northern Ireland, and many others only venture as far as Newry on the borders of Down and Armagh in search of shopping bargains. You may walk for miles through the North's mountains without meeting another soul, while your only companions on some of the glorious beaches will be the seagulls.

Above: Foyle Valley Railway Centre, Londonderry

Below: St. Columb's Cathedral, Londonderry

Crichton Tower, Crom Estate, Co. Fermanagh

Below: The Guildhall, Londonderry

Near Portrush, Co. Antrim

Long Tower Church, Londonderry

Red Bay Castle, Cushendall, Co. Antrim

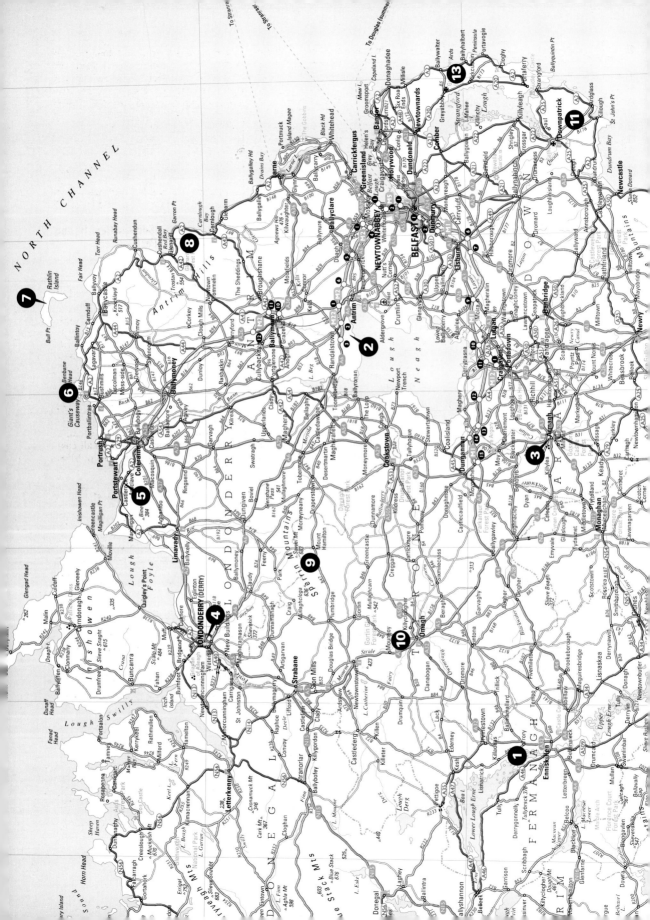

❶ FERMANAGH LAKELAND

The largest lake in this waterland paradise, Lough Erne, is 50 miles long. Apart from fishing and cruising, there are scores of castles, Celtic antiquities and ecclesiastical ruins to investigate. 'Musts' should include Enniskillen; the lavish mansions of Castle Coole and Florence Court; Devinish Island; White Island; Belleek, famous for its pottery; the ancient Marble Arch Caves; and the tranquil Crom estate.

❷ SHANE'S CASTLE

Travel by narrow-gauge railway through the demesne of this O'Neill castle on Lough Neagh's shores. (Open Sun afternoon, April–mid Sep, Wed, June–Aug, and Sat, July–Aug. Phone 084 94 63380) [✆]

❸ ARMAGH CITY

Ireland's ecclesiastical capital. Visit the Church of Ireland and Catholic cathedrals, the ruined Armagh Friary, the Planetarium, the County Museum, and Eamhain Macha, the ancient royal capital of Ulster. *i* 0861 524072

❹ LONDONDERRY (DERRY CITY)

Modern and ancient stand side by side in this walled city. Its walls were completed in 1618. St. Columb's Cathedral, named after the city's founder, was the first built in Ireland or Britain after the Reformation. O'Doherty's Tower is a modern replica of a 16thC castle which stood nearby. Stained-glass windows in the Guildhall illustrate the city's history. The Foyle Valley Railway Centre tells the story of the city's railways. [✆] At Ballyarnett is Amelia Earhart Cottage, commemorating the pilot who landed in a nearby field on the completion of her historic solo Atlantic flight. *i* 0504 267284

❺ DOWNHILL & CASTLEROCK

Outside Downhill is Lion's Gate, one of the entrances to the former demesne of the eccentric Earl-Bishop of Derry, Frederick Hervey, overlooking Castlerock. The Mussenden Temple, perched on a cliff, was his summer library. (Open afternoons, July–Aug, Sat and Sun afternoons, April–June. Phone 025 848281)

Hezlett House is a thatched 17th rectory. (Open daily, July–Aug, Sat and Sun, April–June and Sep)

❻ CAUSEWAY COAST

A few miles from the family resorts of Portstewart and Portrush, the ruins of Dunluce Castle perch precariously on cliffs. The 16thC castle withstood sieges but in 1639 its kitchen, complete with cooks and dinner, fell into the sea. (Open Mon–Sat and Sun afternoon, Mar–Oct) Bushmills whiskey distillery is the oldest legal distillery in the world. (Open Mon–Thu and Fri morning. Phone 026 57 31521) The magnificent Giant's Causeway, formed 60 million years ago, stretches for 4 miles. Its famous columns are a 15 min walk from the visitor centre. (Open daily) The Carrickarede rope bridge will get the adrenalin flowing.

❼ RATHLIN ISLAND

Ireland's largest inhabited island is only 13 miles from Scotland's Mull of Kintyre. It was the site of the first Viking raid on Ireland in AD 795. Robert the Bruce, king of Scotland, hid from the English in a cave below the present lighthouse in 1306. Ferry services operate from Ballycastle.

❽ GLENS OF ANTRIM

Ballycastle, famous for its Old Lammas Fair in August, is flanked by the first glens of Glentaise and Glenhesk. Cushendun is at the foot of Glendun. Cushendall is at the junction of Glencorp, Glenaan and Glenballyemon. Round Red Bay, one of a series of caves above the road was used as a school during the time of the anti-Catholic Penal Laws. Waterfoot is at the entrance to beautiful Glenarrif. Carnlough, at the head of Glencoy, has a picture-book harbour, while Glenarm, the oldest of the villages, is at the tip of the southernmost glen.

❾ SPERRIN MOUNTAINS

This range conceals almost a thousand Stone-Age standing stones, of which the most impressive are the Beaghmore circles between Goirtin and Cookstown. Try gold-mining at the Sperrin Heritage Centre in Cranagh. (Open Mon–Sat and Sun

afternoon, Easter–Sep. Phone 066 26 48142) [✆] The Ulster History Park is at Cullion. (Open Mon–Sat and Sun afternoon, April–Sep, Mon–Fri, Oct–Mar. Phone 066 26 48188) [✆]

❿ ULSTER-AMERICAN FOLK PARK

Replicas of a 19thC emigrant ship, docklands, Ulster village and American frontier settlement, where 'interpreters' re-enact their ancestors' lives. (Open daily, Easter–mid Sep, Mon–Fri, mid Sep–Easter. Phone 0662 243292/3) [✆]

⓫ LECALE PENINSULA

Ireland's patron saint was buried at Downpatrick c. AD 461. His grave is in the grounds of Down Cathedral. Down County Museum is in the former governor's residence and the St. Patrick Heritage Centre is in its gatehouse. The ruins of Audley's Castle on Strangford Lough and the Georgian mansion of Castle Ward (phone 0396 86204) are off the road to tiny Strangford, where ferries cross to Portaferry. In Ardglass, Jordan's Castle is just one of seven small castles which are open to the public. (Open daily, June–Sep)

⓬ MOURNE MOUNTAINS

Newcastle, on the slopes of Slieve Donard, the highest peak, is a good base from which to explore this range. Nearby are the Tollymore and Castlewellan forest parks. Annalong has a working cornmill, and Kilkeel, once the capital of the kingdom of Mourne, is now the home of the area's fishing fleet. Rostrevor is one of the most sheltered places in Ireland and Mediterranean plants thrive here.

⓭ ARDS PENINSULA

Holywood is a yachting centre, while the Ulster Folk and Transport Museum is in Cultra. [✆] Helen's Bay's beaches flank Crawfordsburn Park, and nearby Bangor, a Victorian seaside resort, is still popular. Ballycopeland Windmill, near Millisle, is a working 18thC mill. A fish auction is at Portavogie and the Northern Ireland Aquarium at Portaferry. Greyabbey and Mount Stewart Gardens are on the road to Newtownards.